The Formation of Man

Maria Montessori

AAKAR

The Formation of Man

Maria Montessori

First Published 1949
First Aakar Edition 2020
Reprinted 2021
Reprinted 2023

ISBN 978-93-5002-625-0

Published by
AAKAR BOOKS
28 E Pocket IV, Mayur Vihar Phase I
Delhi 110 091 India
aakarbooks@gmail.com

Laser Typeset at
Arpit Printographers, Delhi

Printed at
Sapra Brothers, Noida.

Contents

PART ONE

Prejudices and Nebulae

Introduction

Contradictions

Almost half a century has gone by since we started our work. The first "Children's House" was inaugurated in 1907 and almost immediately thereafter our ideas and endeavours for child-education spread all over the world. The upheavals caused by two European and world wars during the intervening years have not destroyed this educational movement which has taken root in many countries.

With the passage of time we have become even more convinced of the importance of child-education, and we wish to infuse new life into our endeavour, so that it may become an effective means for the reconstruction of modern society sadly disfigured by the ravages of these worst of all wars in history.

I feel as if I were addressing a strong family which must continue along the road we have opened up and which, young and vigorous though it be, has great need of faith and hope.

I should like to give in these pages a guide for the orientation of our work. Why are there so many difficulties, so many contradictions, so much uncertainty with regard to what are commonly called "Montessori Schools" and the "Montessori Method?" Yet, in spite of this confusion and these difficulties, our schools continue to progress and expand even in the most distant lands. They can be found in the Hawaiian Islands, in Honolulu, in Greenland and in India, among the people of Nigeria, and in Sri Lanka, indeed among all races and in all parts of the world.

Can it be that these schools conducted by African and Indian people, in backward rural areas, or for that matter, in the most civilized nations, are all perfect? Experts say that there is not so much as one good school among them; yet all agree that the Montessori Method is more widely spread than any other modern method of education. How to explain the fact that many nations have changed their educational laws in order not to obstruct the application of the Montessori Method? How did it spread so far afield, without any publicity campaign, when there are only a few regular reviews or organized societies working in harmony with an organic superstructure? It lacked all these aids, yet it spread like a transforming leaven, like the seed propagated by the wind.

Here is another apparent contradiction. The Method seems egoistic, it wishes to go its own way and not to mix with any other and yet, no other method takes every possible opportunity of inculcating world union and world peace as does this one.

All this is contradictory—even mysterious.

Today there are many important currents and personalities in the field of education. There is the New Education Fellowship which wishes to promote harmony between and collaboration with the Montessori Method and the other new methods which continue to crop up. Everywhere this decisive step is looked for to establish an agreement between the efforts of those who in different ways are attempting to educate the child. There is a widespread tendency to break through the isolation of our method, to make students and scientists appreciate it and above all to improve and extend the training of Montessori teachers. I know that many who have dedicated their lives to this Method, now face this problem of cooperation.

Another strange fact about this Method is that though originally worked out for pre-primary education, it has now infiltrated into the primary and secondary stages—even into the University.

In the Netherlands there are five Montessori Lycea, the result of which have been so satisfactory that the Dutch Government has not only granted them subsidies but has given them the same recognition and independence as the other recognized Lycea. In Paris I saw a private Montessori Lyceum where the students were more independent in character and less scared of examinations that in other French Lycea; while in India many people have come to the conclusion that Montessori Universities are a necessity.

In the opposite direction also the Montessori Method has developed, and has been applied to children under three years of age. In Sri Lanka, two-year-old children are being admitted to our schools, while parents request admission for those of one and a half years. In England, many creches follow our Method and in New York also Montessori creches have been founded.[1]

1. In Rome a Training Istitution was founded after the last war where "assistants of infancy" are trained to assist at child-birth, and during the first few years of life, according to the principles evolved by Dr. Montessori from her psychological observations of this most vital phase of development. (Cf. Maria Montessori: *The Absorbent Mind*)–N.O.T.

What exactly, then is this Method, which begins with newborn babies and extends to undergraduates? Other methods have not so wide a function.

For example, the Froebel Method deals with children below school-going age only; that inspired by Pestalozzi is confined to the primary school; while the methods of Herbert deal mostly with primary and secondary education. Among the modern methods we find that of Decroly mostly in primary schools, the Dalton Plan in secondary schools, etc. Traditional methods have certainly been changed, but the teacher of one particular stage cannot teach other grades. No secondary school teacher worries about the methods employed in pre-primary schools, still less about the methods employed in pre-primary schools, still less about those employed in creches. Each stage is clearly defined and the methods, which nowadays are constantly on the increase, are always limited to schools of one or other of these well-defined categories.

To think of Lycea using the Froebel method would be clearly nonsensical. To advocate Nursery School Methods in the University would be equally so.

Why then is the application of the Montessori Method to all stages of education a matter of serious discussion? What does it mean? What is the Montessori Method thought to be?

Constant comparisons and analogies are also being made. The English Nursery Schools, for instance, are being compared to Montessori Schools. The toys used and the treatment of children in the former are being compared to the objects employed and the procedure adopted in the latter, in order to establish some sort of compromise between the two and amalgamate them. In the United States many parallel features have been pointed out in the

Froebelian Kindergarten and the Children's Houses. While comparing the gifts of Froebel and our apparatus it has been pointed out that both are efficient and their conjoint use is advocated. There are only a few conflicting points, e.g. the question of fairy tales, play with sand, the exact use of the apparatus and certain other details about which much discussion is still going on. Also in primary schools the methods of teaching, reading, writing and arithmetic are still being discussed. There is much controversy over our insistence on teaching geometry and other advanced subjects at this early stage. Different opinions are also held regarding the teaching in secondary schools. There are those who think we do not lay sufficient stress on games, and certain activities which give a modern character to teaching methods, by introducing mechanical and manual crafts. Much importance is attached to those questions, as naturally the programme of secondary Montessori Schools has to conform with that of standard secondary schools, otherwise the students would fail to gain admission to the University.

In short, we find ourselves in a maze.

What is the Montessori Method?

One would like to know in a few clear words what this Montessori Method really is.

If we were to eliminate not only the name "Method" but also its common conception, things would become much clearer. We must consider the human personality and not a method of education. For the word "Method" we should substitute something like this: "Help given in order that the human personality may achieve its independence," or "means offered to deliver the human personality from the oppression of age-old prejudices regarding education."

The defence of the child, the scientific recognition of his nature, the social proclamation of his rights, must replace the piecemeal ways of conceiving education.

The "human personality" belongs to all human beings. Europeans, Indians and Chinese, etc. are all men. If therefore, certain vital conditions are found to be a help to the human personality, these concern and affect the inhabitants of all nations.

And what is this "human personality?" Where does it begin? When does a man become a human being? This might be difficult to ascertain. According to the Old Testament man was created as an adult; in the New Testament it is the infant Jesus who appears. The human personality is essentially one during the successive stages of its development. Yet, whatever human being we consider, and at whatever age, whether children in the primary school, adolescents, youths or adults, all start by being children, all then grow from childhood to manhood or womanhood without changing the unity of their persons. If the human personality is one at all stages of its development, we must conceive of a principle of education which has regard to all stages.

In our most recent courses, in fact, we call the child "Man".

Man, the Unknown

Man appearing in this world in the form of a child develops rapidly by a veritable miracle of creation. The new-born possesses neither the language nor any other characteristics which reflect the customs of his kind. He has neither intelligence, memory nor will, not even the power of moving about or keeping himself upright. Yet, this new-born realizes a real psychic creation. At two years of age he speaks, walks, recognizes people and objects in his environment, and at five, he acquires sufficient psychic development to be admitted to a school and start his formal education.

Nowadays, the scientific world is greatly interested in the psychology of the child during the first two years of life. For thousands and thousands of years, mankind had passed the child by, unimpressed by this miracle of Nature–for the formation of the intelligence of a human personality is certainly a miracle. How is it formed? By means of what processes and in obedience to what laws?

If the whole universe is governed by fixed laws, is it possible that the human mind can be formed haphazardly, i.e. without any law at all?

Everything in the course of development passes through a complex process of evolution. Man, too, who at five years of age has become an intelligent being, must have gone through a constructive evolution.

This field, we must admit, has hitherto been unrcplored. There is a vacuum in our present scientific knowldge, an unexplored territory, an unknown factor—and this void concerns the process of the formation of the personality.

The persistence of such ignorance, at the level of civilization to which we have attained, must have mysterious causes. Something has remained buried in the subconscious and an encrustation of prejudices, difficult to break through, has formed over it. In order to start the scientific exploration of this immense and obscure field of the human spirit, we must overcome powerful obstacles. We only know that in the human psyche, there exists an enigma, not yet touched upon by our interest, just as a short time ago we only knew thee was an immense area of ice at the South Pole. Antarctic exploration was then undertaken and a whole continent, full of marvels and wealth, emerged on the horizon of our mind. Its wonders, its warm-water lakes, its large living beings, whose very existence had been unsuspected, now stood revealed. What massive barriers of ice to be broken through and what freezing climate, so different from ours, to be braved. The same applies to that pole of human life— early childhood.

It appears to the adult that he comes from an unknown source. He judges the various aspects of his life as he finds them. His efforts to lead human beings in their successive stages—as children, adolescents, youths, etc.—are therefore empirical and superficial. As a clumsy cultivator he judges appearances and effects without worrying about the causes that produce them. Rightly, Froebel calls the schools for children of four or five years of age "Kindergarten" (gardens of children). It is what all schools could be called—especially the better types where a serious effort is made to benefit the children and promote their happiness. All could be called "gardens" to distinguish them from those schools where only a cruel tyranny reigns. In fact in the more modern and better schools, those that correspond to Froebel's ideas, the educators behave as do good gardeners and cultivators towards their plants.

Behind the good cultivator, however, stands the scientist who scrutinizes the secrets of Nature. His experiments enable him to acquire profound knowledge which helps not only to a better understanding of the plants, but can be used to transform them. The modern cultivator who multiplies the vartieties of flowers and fruits, who reclaims forests, who, we may say, changes the face of the earth, gathers his technical principles from science, not from customary practices. Thus, those marvellous flowers with their varied beauty, those double carnations with all their different hues, those superb orchids, those giant roses so fragrant and without thorns, the many fruits and all the marvels that have changed the face of the earth are the outcome of man's scientific study of plant life. It was science that offered a new technique. It was the scientist who gave the impetus to the construction of a real "supra-Nature" fantastically more rich and beautiful than what we now call "Wild Nature."

The Study of Man

If science began to study man, it would not only succeed in offering new techniques for the education of children and the young, it would further lead to a profound understanding of many human and social phenomena that are still enveloped in obscurity.

The basis of the reform of education and society which is a necessity of our times must be built upon the scientific study of Man the Unknown.

As we mentioned, however, there is a great obstacle to the scientific study of man. This obstacle is formed by the prejudices accumulated during thousands of years and which have become as solid, as majestic and almost as inaccessible as glaciers. A courageous exploration is therefore needed, a struggle against adverse elements, for which the ordinary weapons of science, i.e. observation and experiment, do not suffice.

This study of the spirit of man, of psychology, has grown into an intellectual movement which has spread since the beginning of the 20th century. This discovery of the subconscious has been specially fruitful, first in making contact with adults suffering from mental diseases, and then extending to adults considered normal. More recently child psychology has begun to interest students of this science. The conclusion reached, as a result of these studies, was that almost all men now living have some imperfection in their mental make-up, and statistics irrefutably reveal an ever-growing number of lunatics and psychopathological criminals. They also show that the number of "problem children" is on the increase and stress the growing phenomenon of juvenile delinquency, which is thought-provoking on account of the harm it does to humanity. Evidently the social conditions produced by our civilization create obstacles for the normal development of man.

Our civilization has not yet devised means of defence for the spirit similar to those devised for the body through physical hygiene. While nowadays we control and use the material wealth of the earth and its energies, no consideration has yet been given to that supreme energy represented by the human intellect. While the hidden potentialities of nature have been explored and exploited to their very utmost, the abyss of man's subconscious has not yet been scanned. Man, as a spiritual being, has been left to the mercy of outer circumstances and is on the way to becoming a destroyer of his own constructions.

It is, therefore, possible to conceive a universal movement for human reconstruction which follows a single path. Its sole aim is to help man to preserve his balance, his psychic health and build up a secure orientation in the present conditions of our outer world. This movement is not limited to any one nation nor to any particular political trend, because it aims at the simple realization of human values and that is what is of primary interest over and above all political or national differences.

The conceptions of the old schools, where teaching

continues in the same way as in times profoundly different from ours, are clearly inadequate in view of the aims of the new movement we have outlined above.

Education now becomes a social and human endeavour of interest to all. It must be based on psychology in order to safeguard the individuality of the child. It must furthermore be oriented towards a clear understanding of our civilization so that the personality defended against the disorder of circumstances may become a human being conscious of his real position in history. Evidently a syllabus or curriculum arbitrarily drawn up cannot ensure the culture we need today. There is need of a syllabus which can give an understanding of the conditions of man in modern society with a cosmic vision of history and the evolution of human life. What purpose would education serve in our days unless it helped man to a knowledge of the environment to which he has to adapt himself?

Finally, the problems of education must be solved on the basis of the laws of cosmic order. These laws reach from the eternal laws governing the psychic construction of human life to the changing laws which lead society along the road of evolution on earth.

Respect for these cosmic laws is fundamental. Only when we hold to these as a basis can we judge and modify the multitude of human laws which deal with the passing moments of external social construction.

Our Social Present

It is a commonplace to assert that there exists a lack of balance between the miraculous progress of our environment and the arrest of development suffered by man. Everyone knows that man meets with great difficulties in his adaptation to his environment and that he suffers and deteriorates in the process. We might compare the forces of outer progess to those of a powerful nation which invades and crushes a weaker one and, as always happens in barbaric wars, the vanquished is enslaved.

Today mankind is vanquished and enslaved by its own environment because it has remained weak compared with that environment.

This slavery is growing rapidly and is now assuming forms never experienced in the past struggles between powerful, victorious people, and weak, vanquished ones. never before did human helplessness reach that extreme point witnessed in our days.

Do we not see that nothing is any longer secure? Money kept in banks may in various ways be suddenly and irretrievably lost to its owner and should an attempt be made to safeguard it by hiding it in secret places, as was done in the Middle Ages, it may lose its value and be withdrawn from circulation. The money of one country cannot be taken into another. Even a wealthy person cannot now go to live in the country of his choice for he may not carry money or jewellery across the border. There is the risk of inspection at frontier posts where people are undressed and searched as if their property had been stolen. One can travel only with passports which are now a nuisance instead of a protection as they were originally intended to be. Even in one's own country, one is obliged, specially during a war, to carry about one's photograph and fingerprints—a thing not imposed even on criminals in former days. It happened to us that we were allowed to buy only what was strictly necessary for life and had to depend on coupons distributed at regular intervals to buy even bread. Such a thing was unheard of before, except in the case of mendicants.

Nowadays nobody's life is safe. An absured war may be declared in which all men—young and old, women and children—are in mortal danger. Civilians are bombed and people have to take refuge in underground shelters just as primitive men took refuge in caves to defend themselves against wild beasts. The supply of food may be cut off and millions may die of famine and plague. Do we not see men in rags or even naked, freezing to death, families, separated and torn apart, children abandoned and wandering about in wild hordes?

This we see, not only among those vanquished in war, but everywhere. Humanity itself is vanquished and enslaved—but why enslaved? Because all men are slaves, the victors as well as the vanquished, insecure, frightened, suspicious and hostile, compelled to defend themselves by means of spying and brigandage, using and fostering immorality as a means of defence. Cheating and robbing appear in a changed light and are considered means of survival where restrictions reach an absurd level. Vileness, prostitution and violence become quite common modes of living. Spiritual and intellectual values which once honoured human society lose their bearings. Study becomes an arid, wearying pursuit without any uplifting influence. It is undertaken only as a means to get a job, which in its turn is uncertain and insecure.

It is strikingly impressive that humanity despite its nameless slavery forms a kind of stereotyped chorus crying out that it is free and independent. These miserable and degraded people proclaim their own sovereignty. What do these unfortunates look for? They seek, as their greatest good, what they call Democracy, i.e. that the people may give their opinion as to how they are to be ruled—that they may cast their votes at elections. What irony! To choose one's rulers! But those who rule cannot free anybody from the chains which bind all, which render all activity and initiative futile and render them helpless to save themselves.

The master of all is a mysterious entity. The tyrant is all powerful, like a god. It is the environment that swallows up and crushes the man.

The other days a young baker, who worked in a big mechanized bakery, had his hands caught between the wheels which then trapped his whole body and reduced it to pulp. Is not that a symbol of the conditions in which mankind languishes, unconsciously, a victim of its fate? The environment can be compared to that colossal engine which can produce fabulous quantities of food and the workman it entrapped represents our unwary and imprudent humanity which is grabbed and crushed by what should give it abundance. Here we see one aspect of the lack of balance between man and his environment from which humanity must deliver itself by strengthening its own resources, developing its own values, healing its own madness and becoming conscious of its own power.

Man must gather together all his values and energies, he must develop them and prepare himself for his liberation. This is not the time to fight each other, to try and subdue each other. We must consider man alone and strive to raise him up, to strip him of the useless bonds he creates for himself and which push him downwards into the abyss of lunacy. The real enemy is man's impotence against his own products; it is the arrest of the development of humanity itself. To vanquish this enemy, man has only to react to and behave in a different manner towards the environment, which in itself is a source of wealth and happiness. A universal revolution is what we need. This revolution requires only that man should raise his values and become the master instead of the victim, of the environment he himself has created.

The Task of New Education

It may seem that we have drifted rather far from our original subject—Education. This digression, however, must open up the new road along which we now have to go. In the same way in which we help the patients in a hospital to recover their health and continue to live so we must now help humanity to save itself. We must be nurses in a hospital, as vast as the world itself.

We must realize that the problem in question is not confined to schools as they are conceived today and that it does not concern methods of education more or less practical, more or less philosophical.

Either education contributes to a movement of universal liberation by showing the way to defend and raise humanity or it becomes like one of those organs which have shrivelled up by not being used during the evolution of the organism.

We already mentioned that there is in our day a totally new scientific movement which presents results, at present disconnected—spread here and there—but certainly tending to unify themselves in the near future.

This movement, however, is not really part of education, it belongs rather to the field of psychology. Even in psychology it did not emerge from a pedagogical impulse—to know man in order to educate him—but was rather stimulated by the desire to assuage the sufferings and abnormalities of mankind—especially of adults. This new psychology therefore was born in the field of medicine, not in that of education. This psychology of diseased humanity turned its attention also to children who seemed agitated and unhappy, and it discovered that their vital energies were repressed and deviated from the path of normality.

In any case this is the scientific movement which is taking shape and it aims at building up some barrier against the everspreading evil and at prescribing some remedy for the confused and disoriented soul of man. Education must attach itself to this movement.

Believe me—the attempts of so-called modern education which simply try to deliver the child from presumed repression are not on the right path. To let the pupils do what they like, to amuse them with light occupations, to lead them back to an almost wild state, does not solve the problem. The question is not to deliver man from some bonds, but to reconstruct: and reconstruction requires the elaboration of a "science of the human spirit." It is a patient work, an endeavour based on research, to which thousands of people, dedicated to this aim, must contribute.

Whoever works for this ideal must be actuated by a great ideal, much greater than those political ideals which have promoted social improvements, which concern only the material life of some groups of men oppressed by injustice or misery. This ideal is universal in its scope. It aims at the deliverance of the whole of humanity. Much patient work, I repeat, is needed along this road towards the freedom and "valorization" of mankind.

Look at what happens in the field of other sciences! How many people work in closed laboratories, observing cells under the microscope, discovering the miracles of life. How many spend their lives in chemistry laboratories, testing reactions, discovering the secrets of matter? How many are labouring to isolate cosmic energies in order to capture and use them? It is these innumerable patient and sincere workers who have advanced civilization.

Something similar therefore has to be done for man himself. The ideal, the proposed aim, however, must be common to all. Its realization must lead to what has been said in regard to man in the Scriptures: "*Specie tua et pulchritudine tua intende, prospere procede et regna.*" We might paraphrase it thus: "Understand thyself and thy beauty, proceed prosperously in thine environment, rich and full of miracles, and reign over it."

Now you may say: "Yes, all this is very beautiful and fascinating, but do you not see how, in the meantime, everywhere around us children grow up, young boys become full-grown men? We cannot wait for any scientific elaboration, because meanwhile mankind will be destroyed."

I would answer: "It is not necessary that the whole work of research be accomplished. It is enough that the idea be understood and the work be taken in hand following its indications."

Meanwhile, one thing is clear: Pedagogy must not be guided as in the past, by the ideas which some philosophers and philanthropists formed of it, by some individuals inspired by piety, sympathy or charity. Pedagogy must follow the guidance of psychology, by that psychology which, applied to education, should at once be given a distinct name: Psycho-pedagogy.

Many discoveries have yet to be made in this field. There is no doubt that the liberation of man will give stupendous revelations if he is still repressed and unknown.

Education must proceed along the path lit up by these revelations, just as common medicine is based on the *vis medicatrix nature,* on the curative forces already existing in nature; and hygiene is based on the natural functions of the body.

To help life: this is the first and fundamental principle.

Who then can reveal the natural ways along which the psychic development of man proceeds but the child himself, once he is placed in conditions permitting him to do so?

Our first teacher, therefore, will be the child himself, or rather the vital urge with the cosmic laws that lead him unconsciously. Not what we call the child's will, but the mysterious will that directs his formation—this must be our guide.

I may affirm that the revelations of the child are not at all so difficult to obtain; the real difficulty lies in the adult's old prejudices concerning him. It lies in the total lack of understanding and in the veil which an arbitrary form of education, based only on human reasoning and still more on the unconscious egoism of man and his pride as a dominator, have been weaving, so that the values of wise nature are hidden.

Our contribution—however small and still incomplete—however insignificant in the opinion of those working in the field of scientific psychology—will serve precisely to illustrate this enormous obstacle of prejudices which are capable of cancelling and destroying the contributions of our isolated experience. We would already have conferred a benefit of general importance were we only to succeed in proving the existence of these prejudices.

PART TWO

Prejudices in Science and Education

1

The Revelation of the Natural Order in Children and its Obstacles

Revelations and Obstacles

Let us keep well in mind how our study came into being. About forty years ago a group of four-year-old children revealed an unexpected phenomenon which caused great amazement. This phenomenon was called "the explosion into writing." Some children spontaneously started to write and their example was at once followed by a great number of their companions. There was a real explosion of activity and enthusiasm. Those small children carried the letters of the alphabet in a kind of triumphal procession with shouts of joy. They continued writing without any sign of fatigue or boredom. They covered the floor and walls with their unrestrainable writing. Their progress was really marvellous. Soon afterwards they began to read all types of writing by themselves, cursive script, print, small and capital letters and even special artistic and Gothic lettering.

Now let us examine this first revelation for a while. It was evidently a revelation of a psychological nature and sufficiently powerful to attract the attention of the world at the time. It was a kind of miracle.

Yet what was the reaction, especially of the scientists of the day?

The marvellous writing was not attributed to a psychological fact, but to a "method of education."

Writing and nature could not be associated. Generally, writing is the result of a painful and disagreeable preparation in school. It evokes the memory of dry effort, of pains suffered and punishment inflicted. It reminds us of a torment gone through by all who are not illiterate. The method that had suceeded in obtaining such brilliant results at such a precocious age must, therefore, have been really marvellous. Curiosity arose concerning this method of education which proved to have found at last a means of quickly overcoming the illiteracy which had even lingered on in civilized nations.

When some University professors from the USA came to me to study this method personally, I could not show any other apparatus than the cut-out letters of the alphabet. These letters were objects that could be handled and put here and there, and they were rather large in size.

Some of these professors were offended, and felt that I was making fun of them. In lofty scientific circles, it was being said that all this was not serious. To speak of miracles was a mystification. When it became known later on that instead of books, we used "objects" which could be bought and sold, there was a kind of fear to be mixed up with some commercial enterprise. A kind of *amour propre* withheld the attention of the great from these manifestations which none the less were connected with an unknown factor of a psychological nature. Thus an obstacle was put in its way—*an insurmountable barrier was raised between that illuminating experience and those very people who by virtue of their culture should have been able to interpret and use it.*

Let us pass on to other forms of prejudice.

Those small children who wrote on and on without ever tiring, were a reality which hundreds and thousands of people could see for themselves. Many people had to convince themselves that the letters of the alphabet were simply placed in the environment, each one separate, and that no teacher made an effort to teach the children to write. The children evidently achieved this on their own. Some people consequently began to think that the whole secret lay in the idea of isolating the letters of the alphabet and employing them as movable objects. What a simple discovery of genius! "Why", many of them regretfully wondered, "why did I not think of it myself?" But someone ventured, "This is not a discovery at all. Already in ancient times Quintilian used such a kind of movable alphabet." Had I wished therefore to pose as an inventor and a genius, I would have been shown up then.

It is curious, however, to notice such a widely spread mental inertia, which stops short before an external object without being able, one might say, to go further and consider some new psychological fact with regard to the child. This concerns a real mental barrier common to all, both cultured and uncultured.

Yet it would have been so simple to reflect that if in history the movable alphabet of Quintilian is still remembered, the reactions provoked by it ought equally to have been remembered. Were there processions of enthusiastic people, made with joy, who strode through the streets of Rome carrying banners with the letters of the alphabet on them? Did the people who came in contact with its magic learn by themselves and did they cover the roads and the walls of the houses with written words? Did all learn to read by themselves, and not only Roman script, but

Greak as well? History would certainly have recorded such impressive happenings, but evidently nothing of the kind happened for only the movable letters are remembered. The magic does not lie in them, but in the psychology of the child. At the time nobody would admit to this. That prejudice which forbids us to "believe the extraordinary," the fear of being thought credulous, which is felt by those who wish to uphold their dignity and cultural superiority, is common to all. It is one of the obstacles which hide what is "new" and renders a discovery useless.

A discovery, to be real, must contain something new. This element of novelty is an open door to those who have the courage to go through. It is a door which gives access to hitherto unexplored fields. It is therefore a fantastic, a marvellous door, which ought to strike the imagination. The people of superior culture are really those who ought logically to become the explorers of these fields. A mental and emotional barrier, however, stands in the way of these serious-minded persons, who have lost all relish for the "fairy tales" of Nature. It is extremely rare to find an exception to this rule. Already the famous banquet in the Gospel expressed this eternal fact in symbolic form by implying that a certain degree of simplicity and "poverty" is needed to enter the new realm.

As an example of such barriers we may quote the fate suffered by C.F. Wolff who was the first to discover the construction process leading from a germinal cell to the embryo and ultimately to the hatched chickling. His discoveries met with the concerted opposition of all other scientists of his day, who were involved in the dispute between animalculists and ovulists. They were prejudiced by philosophical theories and would not admit the factual material presented by this young discoverer in his *Theoria Generationis*. He had to leave his country and die in exile. Only fifty years later, when another scientist, K.E. Von Baer, repeated Wolff's investigations, full credit was given to him and the predecessor and then there was born the new science of embryology.

But let it be noted that this recognition was given to a discovery relating to the embryo. Too many prejudices are accumulated, and too many vested interests, where childrenn are concerned. I mean above all the interest created in protecting children from "mental effort," "precocious intellectual activity," etc. In everybody's eyes children are empty beings only suited for play, sleep and the pastime of fantastic tales. Serious mental work done by such young children seem sacrilegious, all the more so after the insistent publications of Charlotte Buhler, the wife of the well known Viennese psychologist Karl Buhler, and herself an authoritative exponent of experimental psychology. Charlotte Buhler reached the conclusion that the mental faculties of children under five years of age are impermeable to any form of culture. Thus, in the name of science, a kind of tombstone was placed over our experiments

The phenomena observed by us among young children were attributed exclusively to a "method of education" which besides was uncertain and disputable. Then the battle of critics began. The discussion concerned above all the question that the mental life of children ought not to be immolated in favour of useless results, because a little later on, after six years of age, all can learn to read and to write and everybody knows at the cost of what effort and sacrifice. We must spare the early years of childhood the painful labour of intellectual study. Claparede, a great authority on pedagogical matters, described on behalf of the New Educaton Fellowship all the damage done to pupils by study in schools. His argument was somewhat as follows: "It is true that our civilization requires study as a necessity but if it harms the child we must try to minimize this harm." The new schools therefore tried to eliminate and have gradually withdrawn from the curricula many subjects not considered necessary, e.g. geometry, grammar and a great deal of mathematics, and substituted games and open air life instead.

Alas, the world of official education too put our work aside! The teachers, moreover, who learned from us at the beginning, were mostly people dedicated to education in the Froebel Kindergarten and thus "gifts" of Froebel were mixed up with our scientific apparatus for mental development and the conclusion reached was that both contained some good parts, but that the alphabet, writing and mathematics should not be introduced into schools for very young children.

Then the teachers of primary schools tried the experiment with the alphabet but they could arouse no enthusiasm nor "explosion" either. The only thing that happened was that a freer form of study slipped into the ordinary schools and that individual occupations and objects were given.

The "miracle" was officially relegated to oblivion. It did not succeed in attracting the test of modern psychology. It was thus left to me to investigate the secrets of child-psychology which this experiment reveals. Nobody better than I could "isolate" these real facts from any educational influence capable of evoking them. It was clear to me that some "energy", peculiar to children at that age, has become manifest and consequently existed.

Even if our experience had been limited to this first group of children, this phenomenon would have been a discovery of powers of the child-psyche which hitherto had been hidden.

Did it not seem a miracle, or perhaps better, a queer occurrence when Galvani saw dead and skinned frogs which had been tied to a window railing, move their legs? If he had thought that he was witnessing a "miracle of resurrection" or an optical illusion, his intelligence would never have persisted in questioning its cause nor would he ever have obeyed its urge to investigate the matter. "If dead frogs move, there must be an energy which makes them do so, ..." he reasoned—and thus electricity was discovered. The development of electricity and its applications went a long distance beyond this revealing phenomenon.

If somebody had wanted to repeat the experiment literally in order to prove it, the miracle might never have been obtained and it would have been thought that the whole thing had been an illusion not worthy of entering into the field of science.

Previous Revelations

Our children were not the first to reveal psychic energies which generally remain hidden. They were, however, the youngest to do so. Previously, similar revelations had been made by children over seven years of age. The history of pedagogy, in fact, gives an account of the "miracles" of the school run by Pestalozzi at Stanz. All of a sudden his wards were enveloped, as it were, by an atmosphere of unforeseen progress. Those children did things considered beyond their age. Some made such progress in mathematics that their parents withdrew them from the Pestalozzi, institution lest they should suffer from mental fatigue. Pestalozzi, in his description of their spontaneous and indefatigable work, followed by such prodigious progress, makes an eloquent confession of the fact that he had nothing to do with these marvellous phenomena. He says, "I was only an amazed onlooker."

Then the flame went out and under the benevolent and affectionate care of Pestalozzi everything returned to normal. It is interesting to know what his admirers, and especially the Swiss, who are so proud of him, thought about it. All of them were of the opinion that the phenomenon at Stanz belonged to a period of craziness in their hero and they rejoiced that he could come back to "serious work."

Thus pedagogy had its triumph by burying a revelation of a psychological nature.

Tolstoy describes something similar about the peasant children he educated with such enthusiasm and affection in the school at Yasnaya Poliana. Suddenly these children began to read the Bible passionately. They came to school in the morning earlier than usual to read alone, without any sign of fatigue. They showed a joy they had never shown before. Then, too, Tolstoy witnessed a "return to normality."

How many similar things, of which we know nothing, must have happened in the lives of children but were unperceived and so remain unrecorded in the history of pedagogy.

The Mental Form of Children

There is, therefore, an inner energy which of its nature tends to manifest itself, but remains buried under universal prejudices. There is a *mental form* peculiar to childhood which has never been recognized.

It was indeed a "mental form" and not only the phenomenon of explosive writing that revealed itself among my children in the first "House of Children" in San Lorenzo.

It happened that when very long words were dictated to them—even foreign words—they reproduced them phonetically with the movable alphabet, having heard them only once. All those, who have read my books know of these phenomena.[1] We dictated, for instance, words like *Darmstadt, Sanglaccato di Novi Bazar, Precipitevolissimevolmente.*

What fixed these complicated words in the minds of the children so that they seemed to retain them with a certainty as if they had been sculptured in their memory? The most marvellous thing was their calmness and simplicity, as if they did not make any effort. It must be remembered that they did *not write*—they had to find each letter in the different compartments of the alphabet-box. One has to look for the compartment of each letter, which is not easy, then take the letter and put it beside the others already in place, so as to complete the word. This would have distracted the attention of any of us.

This astonished the technicians of ordinary education, especially because it is known how difficult dictation is in primary schools. We all know how often a good teacher must repeat every word while the child writes it, even in the case of pupils of eight years and over. The reason alleged is that the child forgets what he is writing. That

1. See *Discovery of the Child* by Dr. Maria Montessori.

is also the reason why at first only short and well known words are given.

Let us recall here the famous anecdote of the Inspector of Schools, Di Donato. Once he came to see our school with a rather severe expression on his face, as a man well armed against possible delusions. He did not wish to dictate long and difficult words, which might hide some trick. He simply dictated his own name Di Donato, to a four-year-old child. This child evidently did not catch the pronunciation well and understood, "Ditonato", so he began to put the third letter down as a "t". The Inspector, faithful to his educational methods, immediately corrected, by repeating his name more clearly. The child was not confused. To him, evidently, it was not a matter of correction or error, but only of not hearing quite distinctly. He took the "t" and instead of putting it back in its compartment in the box, placed it aside on his table. He calmly continued to compose the name and when he came to the end, he took the discarded "t" and used it. The whole name therefore had been impressed upon his mind and the interruption had not created any difficulty. From the beginning he knew that a "t" was needed to complete the word. That was what made such a great impression on the Inspector, who exclaimed, "The mistake was the most eloquent proof of the truth. I confess that I did not believe in this surprising fact, but now I am convinced. I must say, it is incredible, but true." Then without remembering to praise the child whom he had remembered to correct, he turned to me: "I congratulate you." It is not clear that for a technician of education there could be the question only of a "better or worse" method. The psychological fact remained foreign to him. The barrier of prejudice made it impossible for the educator to understand the phenomenon. On leaving, he still thought about it and remarked: "With ordinary methods not even a child of nine could have done that." The compliment was addressed to me.

Yet this incident showed a fact regarding the memory. The thought that there could be a form of memory in younger children different from that of older children could not be conceived. The younger child must have a memory feebler than that of the child five years older.

What, however, was there peculiar in the memory of the young child? Evidently the word, in all its details, was sculptured in his memory. The word, the sounds that compose it and their correct succession remained complete in his mind—nothing could efface them. That memory was of a different nature from that of older children. It created a kind of vision in the mind and the child reproduced this clear and fixed vision with certainty.

The Mneme

Is it then possible that there exists a memory different from that of our conscious and developed minds?

Psychologists of today recognize a form of unconscious memory which retains its fixed images even through generations and minutely reproduces the characteristics of the species. They have given it a distinctive name– "Mneme". The mneme, with its infinite gradations, penetrates into the very facts of life and eternity. Once this has been ascertained, it is easy to recognize in the mind of the four-year-old child a phase of psychic development in which the mneme stands on the very threshold of conscious memory, almost on the point of merging with it, yet manifesting itself as the last trace of a phenomenon with very deep roots.

That last trace of the mneme came from afar. It is linked up with the creative forces of language. The mother tongue was already formed in the unconscious as the result of a process different from that followed by the conscious mind. The mother tongue is the language which is fixed in one's personality as a vital characteristic. It differs from the foreign languages one can aquire with the help of conscious memory—those are always imperfect and can be retained only by constant practice.

The movable letters clearly represent objects that have a bearing on the sounds fixed in the child's mind and they bring his language into the outer world in a tangible form. The interest shown in writing comes from within. A creative sensibility is still vibrating, like that destined by nature to fix the spoken language of man, and from this sensitivity arose such enthusiasm for the alphabet.

The Italian alphabet refers to only twenty-one sounds—yet all the innumerable words, so many that even a voluminous dictionary could not contain them all, can be composed with these twenty-one letters. This alphabet was therefore sufficient to reproduce the patrimony of words which the child has accumulated during his development. It was sufficient to release almost suddenly the explosion of this accumulated language, and the child joyfully lived this miracle.

Discipline

Let us examine another set of prejudices which formed a great obstacle to the understanding of our work.

There was the question raised with regard to "discipline", to the amazing phenomenon shown by those small children who remained orderly and quiet, though they were free to choose their occupations and were not hindered in continuing their exercises as long as they were interested in them.

They were capable of maintaining this orderly behaviour even when the teacher was absent. This collective behaviour, remarkable for its social harmony and the features of their character, which did not show any sign of envy or competition, but led them to help each other, aroused admiration. They "loved silence" and sought it as a real source of joy.

Obedience developed through successive degrees to a high degree of perfection, reaching finally that stage where "obedience was given with joy". There was, I might say, an "anxiousness" to obey, which might remind us of that shown by members of a religious community.

No activity on the part of the teacher was needed to obtain this strange phenomenon. It was, in other words, not a direct result of education, because there were no instructions, no admonitions, neither rewards nor punishments, but everything happened spontaneously.

Yet this unusual fact had to have some cause, it had to be produced by some influence. To those who asked me for an explanation, I could at the time only reply, "It is freedom which produces it," and I had replied to queries regarding the explosion of writing by saying, "It is the movable alphabet."

I remember how a Minister of State, without bothering much about the feature of spontaneity, once said to me: "You have solved a great problem, you have succeeded in fusing together discipline and freedom—this is not a problem which concerns the government of schools only, it concerns the government of nations."

Evidently, in this case also, it was understood by

implication that I had the power of obtaining such results. It was I who had solved a problem. The mentality of people could not accept the other possibility, that the nature of childhood can offer a solution for a problem which we adults cannot solve—that from the child came the fusion of what our mind conceives only as a contrast.

The correct thing to say, in face of such facts, would have been: "Let us study these phenomena, let us work together in order to penetrate into the secrets of the human psyche." But it was impossible for all to understand that from the depths of the child's soul we can draw something new, something useful for all of us, some light that would clarify the obscure causes of human behaviour.

It would be interesting to record the opinions and criticisms voiced on all sides by philosophers, pedagogists and even by the public.

Some said, "You do not realize what you have achieved! You are not aware of the great work you have done!" Others exlaimed, "How can you be so optimistic of human nature?" as if any description of these phenomena were some imaginative tale, or something I had dreamt. The real struggle, which has not stopped yet, was carried on, however, by the philosophers and those religious people who attributed to opinions of mine the facts which so many hundreds of people had witnessed. To some I was a follower of Rousseau. I, evidently, had decided to agree with him that "in man all is good, but everything is spoilt in contact with society." I was supposed to have created in my schools, as Rousseau had done in one of his books, a kind of romantic story.

All the same, in discussions with me, no clear explanation or conviction could be drawn, and a well-known person wrote in an influential paper: "Montessori is a poor philosopher."

According to the religious, I almost went against the Faith and many of them thronged around me to explain the reality of "original sin". It is easy to imagine what Calvinists or Protestants in general thought about it, convinced as they are of the innate and total badness of human nature.

Not only were the principles of the various philosophies concerning the nature of the human soul offended, but the principles of the technique of school education were equally offended, our method was spoken of as aprioristic, as abolishing rewards and punishments and proposing to obtain discipline without these practical aids. It was judged pedagogically "absurd" and to be in contradiction to universal practical experience, even as sacrilegious as it is said that God rewards the good and chastises the wicked, which is for many the most real support of morals.

There was a group of English teachers who protested publicly and declared that if punishments were abolished they would resign from teaching because they could not educate without punishments.

Punishments! I had not realized that they were an indispensable institution holding sway over the entire world of children. All men have grown up under this humiliation.

An inquiry regarding punishments was held by the League of Nations at Geneva, and the Insitut Jean-Jacques Rousseau organized it in cooperation with the New Education Fellowship. Educational institutions and private homes were asked what kind of punishments they used, to educate the children. It is curious that instead of feeling offended at such an indiscreet inquiry all hastened to submit information and some institutions seemed proud of their mode of punishing. Some, for instance, said that immediate punishment was forbidden, lest it be administered in a state of anger, but shortcomings were faithfully recorded and at the weekend, on the sabbath of repose, the dose of punishment deserved for the whole week was administered.

Some families replied: "We are not violent when the child is naughty. We send him to bed without supper."

There is, however, no doubt that violent punishment was very much in favour: slaps, insults, beatings, locking-up, terrible imaginary scares, etc. The list received by the League of Nations in the 20th century was an exemplification of Solomon's proverb: "Spare the rod and spoil the child."

In London, I myself could buy whips sold in bundles, as they were still used by the teachers.

The necessity for these "indispensable" means of education proves that the life of childhood was not and is not democratic and that its human dignity is not respected. From the most ancient times a barrier has been raised in the heart even more than in the mind of the adult. The inner powers of the child have never been realized, neither from the intellectual nor from the moral point of view.

In my experiences the revelations of the child eliminated punishments; yet all this appearing suddenly on account of a fortunate set of circumstances and as an unexpected, yet immediate, revelation, remained incomprehensible to others and caused scandal.

Let me explain by means of an illustration. When something is shown to a dog by pointing the index finger at it with the intention that the dog should go and fetch the object indicated, it will stare fixedly at the finger instead of at the object. It would in the end be more likely that he would snap at the finger instead of going towards the object pointed out to him. The barrier of prejudices in the adult acts in the same way. People looked at me as if I were such an outstretched finger, and in the end snapped at me too.

It was impossible for them to accept simply the evidence of the facts. These facts, in their opinion, had to be somebody's achievement. Somebody had either to produce them or imagine them.

That is why we speak of a blind spot in the heart of man, notwithstanding his capacity to understands so much. This blind spot is similar to that in the retina of the eye, which, nevertheless, is the organ by which all things are seen. The moral vision of the child falls upon the "blind spot" of the human heart and there it strikes a barrier of ice.

We have also spoken of the "blank page" in the history of mankind—that is the page which has never been written—the page referring to the child.

In the colossal and innumerable volumes written on the history of man— the child never appears. Never is he taken into account in politics, in social construction, in war or in reconstruction. The adult speaks as if he, the adult, alone existed. The child belongs to one's private life—it is something claiming duties and sacrifices from the adult and deserves punishment whenever it disturbs him. When the adult dreams of an earthly paradise in a future world, he sees only Adam and Eve and the serpent; in this paradise there is no child.

Our social mentality has not grasped the idea that we can receive help from the child, that the child can give us a light and a lesson, a new vision and a solution for inextricable problems. Even psychologists do not see in him an open door through which they may enter the subconscious. They still try to discover and decipher it through the ills of the adult only.

Order and Goodness

To return to the subject of moral barriers, it was really quite simple to understand the phenomenon of those children's spontaneous discipline and their social behaviour which was so marvellously delicate, sure and perfect.

When we gaze at the stars, twinkling in the sky, ever faithfully following their orbit, so steadfast in their position, do we think: "Oh! how good the stars are!" No, we only say: "The stars obey the laws that govern the universe," and we say, "How marvellous is the order of creation!"

A *form of order* in nature also appears in the behaviour of children.

Order does not necessarily mean goodness. This order does not at all prove that man "is born good" nor that he is born evil. It proves only that nature, in its process of constructing man, follows an established order.

Order is not goodness, but perhaps it is an indispensable way to attain it.

Also our outer social organization needs order as its foundation. The social laws regulating the conduct of citizens and the police force which controls them are of basic necessity in a social structure. Yet a government embodying these institutions can be bad, unjust and cruel. Even war, which is the least good and most inhuman feature of social life, is based on discipline and obedience on the part of the soldiers. The goodness of a government and the discipline it maintains are two distinct things. Similarly, in schools, there can be no education unless discipline is first obtained—yet there can be good and bad forms of education.

Here among these children, order came from mysterious, hidden, inner directives, which can manifest themselves only if the freedom permitting them to be heeded is given. In order to give this type of freedom, it was precisely necessary that nobody interfere to obstruct the constructive spontaneous activity of the children in an environment prepared so that their need for development can find satisfaction.

Before we can reach the point where we are "good", we must first enter into the "order of the laws of nature." Then from this level we can raise ourselves and ascend to a "super-nature" where the cooperation of consciouness is necessary.

Regarding evil and badness, we must also distinguish "disorder" from a descent to a lower moral plane. To be disorderly regarding the natural laws which rule the normal development of the child does not necessarily mean to be "bad". The English, in fact, use different, terms to indicate the "badness" of children and that of adults. They call the former "naughtiness" and the latter "wickedness" or "badness."

We can now state with certainty that the naughtiness of young children represents a disorder regarding the natural laws of psychic life in course of construction. It is not badness but it does compromise the future normality of the psychic functioning of the individual.

Health and Deviations

If instead of normality we say "health" referring to the psychical health of children during growth, everything becomes clearer, as it makes us think of similar facts in the functioning of the body. We say that a body is healthy when all its organs function normally. That criterion applies to all men, whether they are stronger or weak, or whatever their physical temperament may be. If, however, some organ does not function well, we face "functional diseases." These have nothing to do with lesions, with organic diseases. They are the result of abnormal functioning. Such functional diseases can be corrected with the help of hygienic treatment, exercise and the like. Let us carry over this set of conceptions into the psychic field. There too, there are functions that can be disturbed. They do not at all depend on racial characteristics nor on a particular individual type, nor on an ego predestined to great or miserable achievements in life. The genius, as well as the ordinary individual, must have certain functions normally established—he must be psychically healthy.

Now children as they are ordinarily known—unstable, lazy, disorderly, violent, stubborn, disobedient, etc.—are "functionally" ill and can be cured by a hygienic form of psychic life. In other words, they can be "normalized". Then they become like the disciplined children who gave those revelations at the beginning of our work, and who surpised us so much. In consequence of this normalization the children do not become "obedient to a teacher who gives them lessons and corrects them," but they find their guide in the laws of nature, i.e. they start again to function normally. Then they can reveal to us by their outer behaviour that kind of psychic physiology, which, like the physiology of the body, functions within, in the complicated labyrinth of the soul. What is usually called "the Montessori Method" revolves around this essential point.

We can affirm with certainty, after more than forty years of experience, and from repeated proofs obtained among all races all over the world, that spontaneous discipline was the basis on which rested all the other astonishing results, as for example, the explosion into writing and all those other forms of progress which became evident later.

First "normal functioning" must be obtained—a "state of health"— and the establishment of this is what we call "normalization."

If the child is to advance, it is necessary that he should first normalize himself just like a sick man who cannot produce work according to his native endowments unless he first recovers his health.

What psychoanalysts try to do is precisely to "normalize" the adults who find so many difficulties in their activity, in their efforts to achieve their social purpose. In clinics for difficult children the same thing is attempted, namely to bring their functions back to a state of normality.

Let us now suppose that a method of education recognizes that it is necessary to normalize a child right from the beginning and then to keep alive the natural continuation of this state of normality. That method would then have for its foundation a kind of "psychic hygiene" which helps men to grow up in good mental health.

This does not touch philosophical theories regarding the good or evil nature of man—not even the lofty abstract idea of what "normal man" really is. It is a practical fact and endeavour that can be applied universally.

The Basis of Growth

It is all very clear really. A subconscious impulse during the period of growth—that is of the construction of the individual—urges it to realize its growth, and the child is supremely happy when it is simply given the opportunity of doing this and of responding to its urge to make the greatest effort to achieve this. It can be said that the period of childhood is an age of "inner life" which leads to the developing, maturing and perfecting of all the faculties. The outer world has value only insomuch as it offers the necessary means to reach the goal set by nature. That is why the child does not desire anything but what is adapted to its needs and uses it only as long as it helps him to achieve his aim.

Just as the child does not envy a child older than himself, so also he does not desire things which are of no use to him at that particular time.

Hence we observe that peaceful and joyful attitude of the child who, in a favourable environment, chooses his objects and occupations.

The older child cannot inspire the younger one with a desire for competition; on the contrary, this latter's attitude is one of admiration and devotion. For in the older child he sees an image of his own future triumph which is a certainty, because the child will grow if he does not die. The older child does not arouse envy merely by being older.

Those feelings which could be called "bad" do not therefore appear. The naughtiness of small children is a manifestation of defence or of unconscious despair at not being able to "function" during that period on which the whole future depends and every hour of which brings its progress. Naughtiness can also be a form of agitation caused by mental hunger when the child is deprived of the stimuli of the environment or by a sense of frustration experienced when he is prevented from acting in the environment. The "unconscious aim" then moving ever further from its realization creates a kind of hell in the life of the child who becomes separated from a leading source and its creative energies.

It is only much later when the time for "drawing the first sketch of man" is over, and the child, who has been more or less successful in realizing the design of life, begins to be interested in outer things, that envy at the success of others can arise. Things are different then and judgment with regard to "good and evil" can then be made. Then we may speak of defects of a moral order concerning society and the corrective intervention of education can be justified.

Expansive Education

The usual conception of direct correction and suppression of defects is wrong even at this stage. Correction is possible only by expansion of the personality. Wider interests than those observed in another individual at our side must be aroused. Only the poor quarrel over a piece of bread. The rich are attracted by the possibilities offered to them by the world. Envy and competition are signs of "restricted mental development," of a limited outlook. He who has a vision of a "paradise" to be conquered, cannot be satisfied by the whole world and he easily renounces, cannot be satisfied by the whole world and he easily renounces transitory and limited possessions.

The same applies to an education which "amplifed" and leads the individual beyond immediate interests. Envy and struggle are roused by the limitation of what can be conquered. A vast space gives different sentiments—sentiments which engender a passionate devotion for what makes for real progress.

An education of "vastness" therefore is the platform whereon certain moral defects can be eliminated. The first step of education must be to "extend the world" in which the child of today languishes, and its fundamental technique consists in "freeing him from the shackles which impede his advancement." We must "multiply the motives of interest which satisfy the deepest tendencies buried in the soul and bring them within his reach. Invite him to conquer without limits, instead of repressing the desire to possess what belongs to those around him." On this plane, open to the realization of all possibilities, we can, and must, teach respect for the outer laws, established by that other natural power—the society of men.

In conclusion, the moral question, and hence that of moral goodness, cannot be discussed with regard to the "small child." Only when the child comes to the use of reason is it possible to bring the problem of philosophy into the field. Moral philosophers, however, deal with evil in much the same way by directing the individual to transcend its appeals with the aim of reaching God. In fact those who desire to fight against "Original Sin" do so by turning man towards the greatness of the Redemption.

2

Prejudices Regarding the Child in Science and Education

The Acquisition of Culture

In our schools where this educational experience has continued its progress, certain natural tendencies to "extend" culture and "increase knowledge" has become evident in practice. This seems, indeed, to follow the path of Nature. The problems of teaching seem to be reversed there. It appears that the practical problem of the teacher is not to impart knowledge within fixed limits, but rather to "restrain" and "direct" the children in their eagerness to learn ever more, as one has to tame spirited young horses. What is necessary is a guide for this holding back and not whips to make them go on.

The very way of transmitting culture is different. The technique of teaching in ordinary schools is a slow successive progress along supposed difficulties which are graded and classified in advance. Children left free in their prepared environment, on the contrary, revealed original techniques which we could not have suspected.

The child really learns only when he can exercise his own energies according to the mental procedure of nature, and this sometimes works very differently from what is ordinarily supposed. That is why it fails and is hidden when faced with the procedures adopted in ordinary schools. The pupil can show his surprising achievements only if the teacher applies the scientific technique of "indirect intervention" while helping the natural development of the child.

The precocious and extensive cultural progress revealed by our children which called forth such admiration but also scuh opposition based on misunderstanding, and a lack of understanding, rests on a principle referring to the psychology of the child. This is, that the child learns by his own activity, taking culture from the environment and not from the teacher, and further, as can now be satisfactorily proved, by putting into action also the powers of the subconscious which remain free to absorb and express according to the natural processes of the absorbent mind.

It will be said that the teacher forms part of the environment, and in fact he intervenes by helping this natural process, yet the fact remains that the child cannot, as is generally believed, learn only through the efforts of the teacher who explains things, even if he is the most excellent and perfect of teachers. Also in learning the child follows inner laws of mental formation. There is a direct interchange between the child and his environment while the teacher with his offerings of motives of interest and his initiations constitutes primarily a link, a *trait d'union* between them.

The process of learning has been gone into ever more deeply since our experiences were intensified, with the intention of getting to know these phenomena more intimately. It was found among many children placed in suitable conditions that they were passionately interested in mathematics, in big numbers, and not only in big arithmetical operations, but also in calculations on quite a superior level, like those on the powers of numbers, the extraction of square and cubic roots—and especially in geometrical problems. We also discovered their capacity for learning several languages at the same time, studying the grammar and style of each. There was for example an eight-year-old child in India who took great interest in reading Sanskrit poetry, though Sanskrit is a dead language, and translated Vedic stories from Hindi into English although his mother tongue was Gujarati—another Indian language. His culture, therefore, extended from living and dead languages to those of a foreign country.

To this may be added their interest in natural science, their prodigious memory for names and, curiously enough, their delight in learning complicated systems of classification of plants and animals. These classifications are often not only uncertain, but seem to encumber the memory unnecesarily and official science is therefore thinking of abolishing them at least from school syllabuses, considering them as demanding useless effort.

This interest in "classification" revealed itself with the help of movable symbols. The pleasure experienced by children, when they could create a mental order among these pictures and put each in its own place, was very evident. It certainly was not an exercise of the memory, but one of construction similar to that of a small child who plays with wet sand. The many ideas and names which would otherwise be "lost" to the memory are gathered and captured in a fascinating construction. It is rather like the mathematical apparatus which is built up in the exercises of the decimal system, where units are gathered in such clear successive hierarchies that arithmetic is almost a consequence of the order of units. Thus it happens also with historical events placed in relation to their dates and to geography which constructs in the mind a system of cultural facts in time and space.

The creative forces of nature also proceed in this way. In the construction of the mother tongue by the child, language is initially built up on the sounds of words and on grammar, i.e. the order in which the words have to be placed to express thought. This is the first fundamental construction which is completed shortly after the child has reached two years of age, while the number of words is still comparatively small. Afterwards language is enriched spontaneously by new words, which find their places in the order already established.

We found that the procedure adopted by us, with children under nine years of age, could be applied to those of more advanced age, and we can affirm that at all stages of school life it is essential that no obstruction be placed in the way of the individual activity of the children in course of development. Only thus can they obey the "natural process of psychic development". It is true that the teacher or lecturer has an ever more important role to play as culture reaches higher levels, but this role consists rather in stimulating interest than in actual teaching. When children are interested in a subject they tend to spend a long time studying it, or in other words, trying to find their own experience. After that an acquisition has not only been made, but it tends to extend itself ever further. The teacher then finds himself compelled to go beyond the limits he had put to his own teaching. His difficulty then does not lie in how to "make the pupils learn", but in knowing how to meet unexpected claims on the part of his pupils, in having to teach, then and there, things he never intended to teach. Instruction, in other words, tends to extend of its own accord. Often, after a long rest, say a vacation the children do not merely retain what they had previously learnt, but their culture seems to be richer as if by magic. After the holidays they know more than before. Their power to absorb from the environment has therefore been reawakened.

The procedure of spontaneous activity consists sometimes in a voluntarily intensified and complicated effort which absorbs all their mental energies for hours on end and even during several consecutive days. I remember a child who wanted to draw a river— the Rhine—with all its tributaries. He had, therefore, to search a long time in geographical treatises which had nothing to do with school books. For the actual drawing he chose graph paper as used by engineers, and made use of compasses and various other instruments. He succeeded in his endeavour showing tremendous patience—nobody, surely, would ever have exacted such an effort from him.

Another time I saw a boy who had resolved to work out a gigantic multiplication of a number consisting of 30 figures by another of 25 figures. The partial products accumulated to such an extent that the boy was surprised. He had to have recourse to the help of two friends who had to find sheets of paper and stick them together to contain this monstrous operation and its enormous development. After two consecutive days of work the multiplication was not yet finished. It was completed only the next day, yet without the boys showing any sign of being tired of it. They, too, seemed proud of and satisfied with their great achievement.

Again, I remember four or five children who decided to carry out together the algebraic multiplication of the whole alphabet by itself: to work out the square of the alphabet. This time also, the operation required the material effort of sticking together ever more strips of paper, which in all reached a length of about ten metres.

These patient endeavours lead to a strengthening of the mind and render it more agile, as gymnastic training does to the body.

Once a child acquired the capacity to carry out quite complicated operations with fractions, without writing them down. He thus showed his ability to retain in his mind the image of the numbers and the successive operations. While the child carried out these operations mentally, a teacher did so on paper, not being able to do them otherwise. At the end of his calculation the child announced his result. The teacher (who was in chage of a number of English schools and had come to visit our schools in the Netherlands) remarked that the result given by the child was not correct. The child, without being perturbed in the least, thought for a while and then said: "Yes, I see where I made a mistake," and gave the correct result somewhat later. This subsequent mental correction in quite a complicated calculation caused greater astonishment than the fact that he had been able to carry out the operation itself. The mind of the child, evidently, possessed a peculiar faculty for retaining all these successive phases.

Yet another time, there was a child who had learnt the extraction of the square root according to the procedure indicated by our apparatus. He was intensely interested in extracting such roots by himself, but he did so in a different way invented by himself, which, however, he could not explain.

We could go on giving endless examples. One of the most extraordinary ones was the patient work of a boy who wrote down the grammatical analysis of a whole booklet. He never interrupted this work until it was completed and spent several days doing nothing else.

These psychic manifestations reveal a kind of formative mechanism expressed by exercises without any outer utility, without any practical applicability. It would not be possible to impose them as one can do in physical drill, because it would be impossible to sustain from without such a lively and uninterrupted interest, such a constant attention for things which in themselves are not very attractive and rather purposeless.

They require really a spontaneous effort such as would be impossible to inspire from without. Notwithstanding such a "waste of time" shown by so many children in various occupations these same children make exceptional progress in all the branches of culture and also in art. In a school in India, where there was a special teacher for music and dancing, a group of children often gathered in the music room when that teacher was not there and improvised dances which the teacher had not taught them. They differed very much from the rigidly prescribed movements of classical Indian dancing. Various children would play on instruments rhythms which accompanied a kind of choral singing invented by themselves. All showd an intense interest which was more than mere delight. From time to time these unexpected forms of music were heard in the school.

We encounter here phenomena very different from those considered in ordinary education and in educational psychology, which is concerned only with will and effort. These are considered as results of reflections of the intellect or of external compulsion. Here, however, we witness a kind of *élan vital,* and eruption of unforeseen and unsuspected manifestations which have nothing to do with reflection nor with any practical or utilitarian application. Nevertheless, progress in a real acquisition of culture is evidently much more helped by these inner energies than by a voluntary and imposed effort. The results thus obtained are not directly related to these strange exercises of patience and this constant work. They seem to belong rather to inner mechanisms which by their action give an impluse to the development of the personality as a whole.

In fact one of its most dindirect consequences is the formation of "character". The children not only make progress in a marvellous acquisition of culture, but they acquire more mastery of their actions, more assuredness in their behaviour, without any stiffening or any hesitation due to timidity or fear. They are also ready to adapt themselves to other people and to the environment and its different exigencies. Joy in life together with discipline seems to be more the result of their activities guided from within than from any outer circumstances. On this basis the children are then prepared to master the environment. As they are more balanced and more capable of orienting and valuing themselves, they are characteristically calm and serene, and for that reason also easily adapt themselves to other people.

In the course of our experiences we met with crushing opposition by prejudices on this point also. Although all complained of the lack of culture and emphasized its absolute necessity for civilized life in our times, yet there was great opposition to the development of culture in our schools. It seemed almost as if the child has to be defended against us. The forces of mental inertia considered these revelations of the children almost as a pedagogical and still more as a psychological heresy and vigorously opposed the presentation of our apparatus which helped such development. The discoveries of mental *surmenage,* strain, among children in ordinary schools were brought into the field and we were accused of forcing the intellectual energies of the child. Our so-called intellectualism was denounced, while we ourselves were absolutely innocent of it all.

The simple facts, of which we have related only a few, surprised us as much as they did others, but in the case of these latter, their surprise was mixed with suspicion. Who would ever have claimed to evoke the manifestation of these powers in the children? Certainly not I! The children themselves revealed them and we did nothing but respect them in the atmosphere of the freedom of our schools. We responded only with the help they sought. We did, however, make an attempt to understand the source of these powers, and to investigate the conditions which permitted and perhaps facilitated their "eruption". Only the universal repetition of the same phenomena, moreover among children of so many different races and of civilizations so much more primitive than ours, compelled us to conclude that we were face to face with "normal" possibilities, with truly human powers which all too long had remained hidden on account of a lack of respect for the laws of psychic development on the part of the adult. They had remained unknown because the adult had denied them the help which it is their right to claim from education.

The Social Question of the Child

The results we have touched upon are not easy to obtain because enormous obstacles are encountered in century-old prejudices. The field of child-life and child-education is one in which all have had experience right from the beginning of man's appearance on earth, and in which they continue to have experience. These experiences have had a long time to consolidate and to become universal. Unfortunately there are also modern branches of science or attempts at science, which have developed around the most superficial manifestations of child behaviour (actually around the "effects" of outer circumstances) and these reached an easy compromise with those prejudices which every adult cherishes regarding the child. That is why the manifestations of child-life which we mentioned are not observed by people "who have eyes and see" but by those already blinded by prejudice.

These prejudices are so universal that it is difficult to have them recognized as such. They are confused and strengthened by the evidence of facts because all, or nearly all, see the child as he is commonly recognized, not the child as he is, still an unknown entity. In fact if one should tell an audience that in order to reform education many prejudices have to be overcome, the most progressive and unbiased among the listeners would think at once of prejudices relating to what has, or has not, to be taught and not of prejudices regarding the child himself. They think that it is a question of removing prejudices and errors from what is taught, so as not to transmit them to the younger generation. Some hold that the teaching of dogmatic religious conceptions should be avoided; others again that certain formal habits no longer belonging to our society should be eliminated, and so on.

It seems, however, as yet, inconceivable that there are prejudices which "prevent" us from seeing the child from a point of view different from that which is usually taken of him.

Yet those who study child-psychology and education must take into account, not those social prejudices which bother modern educationists so much, but other prejudices—those which concern the child directly, his natural attributes and powers, the abnormal conditions of his life.

By removing religious prejudice, it may perhaps be possible to understand better the greatness or significance of religions but not the natural personality of the child. By removing prejudices concerning social castes it may be possible to intensify the understanding and harmony between the members of society, but it will not help to a better understanding of the child. If many formalities in our social relations are recognized to be futile, belonging to the past, we may witness a reform of social customs but we will not understand the child any better.

All that seems to contribute to social progress among adults can, according to common opinion, leave the vital necessities of childhood aside. The adult has always seen only himself in sociey—an unknown quantity in the equation of life.

Hence a prejudice has found its way into the adult—the notion that the life of the child can be changed or improved only through teaching. This prejudice impedes the understanding of the fact that the child constructs himself, that he has a teacher within himself and that this inner teacher also follows a programme and a technique of education, and that we adults by acknowledging this unknown teacher may enjoy the privilege and good fortune of becoming its assistants and faithful servants by helping it with our cooperation.

Many other prejudices are the logical consequences of this one. It is said that the mind of a child is empty—without a guide and withut laws of its own. Adults, therefore, are supposed to have the great and complete responsibility of filling it, guiding and commanding it. It is believed that the child is naturally inclined towards a number of defects, towards decadence and inertia, that by nature it is blown hither and thither as a feather driven before the wind, and that adults, therefore, must stimulate and encourage him, correct and guide him all the time.

In the same way it is assumed in the physical order that the child cannot control his movements and is incapable of taking care of himself, and so the adult hurries to do everything for him without bothering to consider that the child can very well manage alone. The child is then said to be a heavy burden and a great responsibility as he requires this constant care. The attitude of the adult to the children is that he must "create" in him a grown-up man and that the intelligence, the socially useful activity, the character of this human being, who has entered his home, are all his work.

Then pride is born as an accompaniment to this anxiety and sense of responsibility. The child seen in this light owes infinite respect and gratitude to his creators, his saviours. If, instead, he rebels he must be corrected, must be brought into submission with the help of violence, if necessary. In order to be perfect, the child must then be perfectly passive and most rigorously obedient. He is a perfect parasite of his parents and as long as these assume the whole economical burden of his life, he must depend upon them absolutely. He is a "child". Even when he has grown up and has to shave regularly each morning before attending the University, he still remains dependent on his father and teachers just as when he was still a child. He must go where his father wishes him to go, study, often, as his teachers and professors wish him to study. He will remain outside society even when he takes his degree and may be 26 years of age.

He cannot marry without his father's consent till quite an advanced age which has been fixed, not in consideration of his needs and sentiments, but by a social law promulgated by the adults and equal for all.

He must actually obey unto death, when society tells him: "Parasite, prepare yourself to kill or be killed!" If he does not do that, if he does not render military service, he will be ostracized from society and classed as a delinquent.

All this runs through our world like the quiet water of a brook through a meadow. This is the preparation for life given to a man; and as for women, they are still more dependent and condemned for life.

The norms of this way of life form the basis of society. Nobody may be called good who does not submit.

Thus from birth onwards and till all the rules dictated by the adult have been followed, the child and youth are not considered as men in society. They are exemplified by those young students who are told: "Think of your studies. Do not occupy yourselves with politics and ideas different from those which have been imposed upon you. You have no civil rights."

The social world is opened only after this kind of

dictatorial preparation.

We must admit that some evolution has taken place during the history of civilization. While Roman Law recognized the father as master of his family with the right to kill his children as he created them by a right of nature and while, in those days, weak or deformed children were destroyed by being thrown down a steep rock (the Tarpeian rock) which fulfilled the function of purging the race, Christianity, on the other hand, placed one's own child and the deformed child under a law of respect for life. That however, is all. The child can no longer be killed.

Slowly science in the shape of hygiene has succeeded in "protecting" the life of the child against disease and evident cruelty. It has, however, taken great care not to dictate how to reform social conditions so that the life of all children, and not of the diseased ones only, be protected.

The personality of the child has remained buried under the prejudices of order and justice. Though the adult has agitated very strongly in defence of his own rights he has overlooked those of the child. He is not even aware of him. On this plane, life has continued to evolve and to complicate itself up to the 20th century.

From the complex whole of such conceptions arise the particular prejudices which impose themselves under the cloak of so praiseworthy an aim as the protection of, and respect for, the life of childhood.

The small child, for example, should not be let to do any form of work. He must be abandoned to a life of intellectual inertia. He should only play in a certain well-established way.

If, therefore, one day it is disccovered that the child is a great worker, who can apply himself to his work with concentration, who can learn by himself, this seems to be like a fairy tale. It does not evoke surprise, it just appears utterly absurd.

No attention is paid to this reality, and hence no conclusion is reached to the effect that in this apparent contradiction may be hidden an error on the part of the adult. It is simply impossible, it cannot exist—or as it is said, it is not serious.

The greatest difficulty in the way of an attempt to give freedom to the child and to bring its powers to light does not lie in finding a form of education which realizes these aims. It lies rather in overcoming the prejudices which the adult has formed in his regard. That is why I said we must recognize, investigate and fight against "the prejudices concerning the child" only, without touching other prejudices which the adult may have formed regarding his own life.

This struggle against prejudices is the social question of the child which must accompany the renewal of its education. It is, in other words, imperative ro prepare a positive and well-defined route leading to this goal. If the prejudices concerning the child are directly and exclusively aimed at, a reform of the adult will accompany it step by step because an obstacle in the adult will have been removed. This reform of the adult is of enormous importance for society as a whole. It represents the reawakening of a part of human consciousness which has been covering itself progressively with layer upon layer of impediments. Moreover, without this awakening all other social questions become obscure and the problems raised by them insoluble. "Consciousness" has been dimmed, not in some adults only, but in all adults—because all have dealings with children. As their consciousness is dimmed regarding the child, they also act unconsciously. On this point they do not use their powers of reflection, their intelligence which leads them to make progress in other fields. There is in them, as we already mentioned, a blind spot, similar to that on the retina of the eye. The child, that unknown being, that only apparently human being, sometimes considered almost as a matrimonial accident, who opens a road of sacrifices and duties, does not in himself arouse either awe or admiration.

Let me describe a psychological complex. Suppose that in nature the child appeared to be a divine miracle, of the sort men feel in the presence of the image of the child Jesus, which inspires artists and poets and represents the hope of redemption for all mankind, an august figure at whose feet the kings of the East and West devoutly place their gifts. This child Jesus is also, however, amid the religious worship paid to him, a real child, a newly-born babe without consciousness. Almost all parents feel similar lofty sentiments at the birth of their child, who is idealized by the strength of their love. Later, however, as this child grows up, he begins to be a nuisance. Almost remorsefully they begin to defend themselves against him. They are happy when he is asleep and try to make him sleep as long as possible. Those who can, hand their child over to the care of a nurse and, taking courage, instruct her to keep him away from them as much as possible. If this unknown and incomprehensible being, acting in obedience to unconscious urges, does not submit, he is punished, fought against, and being weak and defenceless both intellectually and physically, he must bear all. In the adult's soul there occurs a "conflict" bcause he does love the child. At first this conflict causes pain and remorse. Later, however, the psychic mechanism at play between the conscious and subconscious in man reaches a form of adaptation. As Freud would say, there occurs a fugue. The subconscious prevails, i.e. it suggests, "What you do is not in order to defend yourself against the child, it is a duty you perform in his regard. It is a necessary good. You must even act bravely because you are 'educating' the child. You are striving to build up goodness in him. When this comfort is obtained, the natural feelings of admiration and love are effectively buried."

This is seen in all, because this phenomenon belongs to human nature. Thus a kind of "subconscious organization of defence" is achieved by all parents in the world. All lean upon each other. The whole of society forms a collective subconscious wherein all act in complete agreement when they remove and suppress the child. They all act for his good, they all perform a duty towards him, in fact, even a sacrifice, In this way, that kind of remorse, which was there originally, is sacrificed. In this conflict it remains definitely buried under the solidarity of adult society. What has thus been established assumes the power of suggestion and the appearance of an absolute truth on which all agree. Future parents, in their turn, are subjected to this suggestion and prepared for the duties and sacrifices they will have to perform for the future well-being of their children.

These people who are victims of suggestion prepare their consciousness for such an adaptation, and the child is buried in the subconscious. As in all people who are victims of suggestion, in these too, there exists henceforth only what has been established by suggestion. This state of affairs is perpetuated from generation to generation.

In the course of ages, the child, buried as he is, will no

longer be able to reveal anything of his lofty nature.

We have given a kind of formula—an acrostic—to indicate this phenomenon. What is believed to be good is in reality disguised evil. This evil has organized itself and has found a subconscious solution for grave conflicts. Nobody desires evil, all desire good, but that good is evil. Everyone has been infected by it through the suggestion coming from the morally uniform environment. In society, therefore, an Organization of Evil (*Male*) has been which assumes the semblance of Good (*Bene*) and is imposed on the whole of humanity (*Umanta*) by Suggestion; when we combine the initials of these characteristic words and form a word, we then get: OMBIUS.

The OMBIUS

The social ombius dominates the child. All submit to it instead of seeing the sublime child as the little brother of the child Jesus. Ombiotic feelings fatally cover the life of the child while a luminously ideal figure of him remains as a symbol only on the altars of religion.

When adults come to the sincere conclusison that all are children of God and that Christ lives in each one of them and he becomes their model for imitation, or better still, for identification with him to the extent of being able to say: "I live now, not I, but Christ liveth in me," they except the child. The child Jesus remains separate from the poor newly-born, who is buried under the ombius. In him, people see only the original sin which must be fought against.

This short illustration based on the psychological secrets of human nature shows the primordial reality of growing and total oppression of the child. The prejudice of the whole of society, organized by the adults, weighs upon him, although he is isolated in the family. In the course of evolution and the successive social movements for the rights of man, the child is forgotten.

The history of the injustices committed against the child has not yet been written officially and is, therefore, not taught as part of the history studied in schools of any grade. Even students who take a specialized degree in this subject have never heard it mentioned. History deals only with the adult because only he exists in our consciousness. Similarly those who specialize in legal studies learn a number of laws both of the present and past but they never become aware that no laws have been promulgated on behalf of the child's rights. Civilization ignores a question which has never yet become a "social problem."

Yet the child is taken into consideration when he can be of use to the adult, but even then he continues to touch the blind spot of consciousness as far as his destiny as a human being is concerned.

Let us take the most evident example. At the time of the French Revolution the "Rights of Man" were proclaimed for the first time. Among these was included the right of all men to be taught how to read and write. What was till then a privilege most readily accessible only to members of the better classes became now a universal right. It would have been logical had all adults availed themselves of this opportunity even though it entailed an effort, because here was a right which not only did away with exclusive privileges but also implied an effort to improve the individual.

However, the burden of this was laid only on the children. On them the whole burden of the effort required to make this conquest was laid.

Thus we see here, for the first time in history, a

"mobilization" of children, both boys and girls. All were equally called up for service in the schools, as in time of war manhood is mobilized for military service in the field.

We all know the lamentable story. The child was condemned to a life sentence because for the whole of his life as a child he was sent to prison. Locked up within bare cells, kept sitting on wooden benches, under the sway of a tyrant who insisted that the children should think as he wished, learn what he wished and do what he wished. The delicate hand of the child was made to write. His mind, full of imaginative powers, had to concentrate on the dry shapes of the alphabet which did not reveal to him any of the advantages which its possession confers upon us. These advantages are discovered only by the adult.

What a history of unrecorded martyrdom! Children were tortured—their figures tied to penholders; they were beaten with rods and forced to do cruel exercises. The sufferings of these little prisoners are too well known—even their spinal cords were twisted and deformed by being condemned to sit on wooden benches for hours on end, day after day, year after year, and that during the delicate years of early growth.

Herded together, exposed to the promiscuousness of diseases, suffering from the cold—it was thus children had to live in those concentration camps. This lasted up to our century. The advantage derived from this situation was a right belonging to the adult, not to the child. Nobody, however, felt any gratitude towards him, nobody tried to alleviate his sufferings. Yet there always lived on in parents those natural feelings of parental love which they showed at the birth of their child. Always too there were those instincts for the protection of the young, common even to animals.

How can this be explained except by a mysterious phenomenon in our consciousness? What could explain better than this example the reality of the ombius and the prejudices concerning the child?

Now in our century a serious effort is being made to alleviate those sufferings. An attempt is being made to transform education. More healthy and beautiful schools are being built. All this, however, is being effected around the same image of the misunderstood child who is still seen through eyes distorted by the ombius.

3
The "Nebulae"

Man and Animals

Only when we consider the newly-born human child logically do we see that he differs from the newly-born of mammals, from the point of view of heredity. The young of mammals inherit, as all animals generally do, specialized behaviour. This is as fixed as the morphological features of their body. The bodily form is precisely suited to the functions it has to perform in life. These functions are fixed for each species. The habits, the way of moving, whether of skipping, running or climbing, are established from birth onwards. Their adaptation to the environment, therefore, aims at exercising characteristic functions, the purpose of which is not merely to preserve the species, but further to contribute to the total functioning of nature which is their cosmic purpose. The legs of those which jump, run, climb or dig into the earth are formed in such a way as to correspond to the task of each. Also ferocity or the avidity to feed on corpses and offal contribute to the cosmic order on the surface of the earth. In short, the body in its fleetness or rigidity is built so that the "cosmic aim" of each individual species may be fulfilled. The species endowed with the power of some particular limited variability of innate adaptation are very few. Those species have all been domesticated by man. The greater part of the animals preserve an absolute rigidity in their hereditary characteristics and cannot be domesticated.

Man, on the contrary, has an almost unlimited power of adaptation regarding his capacity to live in all geographical regions, and his capacity to assume innumerable forms of habit and work. Man, in fact, is the only species capable of an indefinite evolution in his activities in the outer world. From this flows the development of civilization. The human species is the only one which by nature is not fixed in its behaviour as all other species are. It is, as biologists recently asserted, a species in a perpetual state of infancy, because it develops in continuous progress.

This, therefore, is the first difference—man does not receive an inheritance of fixed behaviour.

Another evident difference is that no young of a mammal is born as inert, as incapable of actualizing the characteristics of the adults, of its species, as is the newly-born human being. Many animals such as kids, foals and calfs stand on their own legs almost at once and during the period of lactation they run after their mothers.

Even monkeys, which are considered nearest to man, are vivaccious and intelligent as soon as they are born, They cling energetically to their mothers of their own strength and need not be carried in their arms. The mother monkey climbs trees while her young holds on to her, gripping her tightly with its little arms. Not only that, but often the young one tries to run away and the mother must make an effort to catch it and keep it with her.

The human child, instead, is inert for a long time. He does not speak, whereas all other young creatures at once begin to chirp or bark or reproduce the sound peculiar to their species. All dogs the world over, of whatever breed they may be, bark. All cats mew just as all birds have their peculiar cries and songs—a form of expression belonging to the characteristics of their species.

The long inertia and incapacity of the child belong truly to the human species alone. At an age when a bull is capable of reproduction although it has a body so much larger than that of a man, and more or less the same physiological organs, the child is still a mere child far from maturity.

Those who study only the evolution of the morphological form and its respective organs in order to deduce from it the direct descent of man from animals, have, however, given insufficient attention to the differences which are thrown into relief by this mysterious feature of the length of human childhood. Thus a void remains which the theories regarding evolution have not yet considered.

It would, in fact, seem possible to agree on a logical basis that man is, physically, an ape, evolved by means of long efforts at adaptation to the environment and through those efforts only, because there is an evident similarity between the body of man and that of the ape. The face and skull of a primitive man resemble very much those of a superior ape. The limbs and generally the skeletons of both are suprisingly similar. Those who think that primitive man had also to climb trees like a monkey are merely insisting on a commonplace which has been fantastically elaborated in the motion pictures of "Tarzan". Yet one thing remains inexplicable. We can imagine a primitive man of low morphological type, who climbed trees, but we cannot admit that such men had newly-born infants who spoke, clung to their mothers of their own strength, got to their feet and immediately started to run about. It is difficult to give reasons why man as he evolved to superior types of life, i.e. towards the species of the *homo sapiens*, should seen his infants become passive, dumb, deprived of intelligence and for years on end incapable of achieving what they could do in previous stages of evolution. One of the characteristics, therefore, of human beings, which is distinctly different from those found elsewhere, resides in the newly-born child.

It does not matter that we cannot today explain this fact. The fact is there and makes it easy to argue that, if the newly-born child of man is so evidently and greatly inferior to that of the mammals, he must have a special function which the others do not share.

This function does not come from the inheritance of previous infantile forms. It is, therefore, related to some new character which has arisen during the process of evolution.

This character cannot be recognized by observing the adult human being, but it is clearly seen by observing the child.

Something new occurred during the evolutionary process which led to the development of man, just as new characteristics also occurred in the animal world when, after the reptiles, birds and mammals came into existence, i.e. warm blood and an instinctive care for the preservation of the species. The true difference between birds and reptiles does not lie in the matter of teeth in the beak of the archaeopteryx, or the long tail made up of many vertebrae, but in the parental love which did not exist before and which appears together with the warm blood. These are, therefore, additions in evolution, not merely transformations.

The Function of the Child

The child must have a special function besides being merely smaller and weaker than the adult. He does not possess "by birth" all the attributes which are destined to increase and grow within him as a means to attain adulthood. Actually, if he already possessed such fixed features, as happens in other species, man could never adapt himself to such different places and habits, nor evolve in his social manners, nor take up such different forms of work.

He is, therefore, different from animals precisely with regard to heredity. He evidently does not inherit characteristic features, but only the potentiality to form them. It is, therefore, after birth that the characteristics, proper to the particular kind to which the child belongs, are built up.

Let us take language as an example. It is certain that man must possess and transmit hereditarily the completely new faculty of developing a language which is related to intelligence and the necessity of transmitting thought for the purpose of social cooperation. Yet there does not exist any particular language which is thus transmitted. Man does not "speak a language" merely because he grows, as a puppy barks wherever in the world it is found, even if isolated from other dogs. Language is developed gradually, precisely during that epoch of inertia and unconsciousness of early infancy. At two years or two years and three months, the child speaks distinctly and reproduces precisely the language spoken in his environment. He does not by heredity reproduce the language of his father and mother. In fact, if a child is taken from his parents and people and reared in another country where another language is spoken he will reproduce the language of the place where he lives. If an Italian baby is taken to the USA, he will speak English, with an American accent, and will not know Italian. It is, therefore, the child himself who assumes a language, and till he acquires it he is dumb in contrast to the young of other animals.

Those "jungle-children" of whom history speaks were children found abandoned in the forest. Through exceptional circumstances they had survived abandonment in the midst of wild animals and they were mute even at the age of twelve or sixteen years when they were first discovered. None of them reproduced the cries of the animals amongst which they had lived and by which they were adopted in a certain sense. The famous savage of Aveyron was mute when at the age of eleven he was found and then educated by the French physician Itard who discovered that the boy was neither deaf nor incapable of speech. In fact he learnt to speak French and also to read and write it. He had remained deaf and dumb in appearance only because he had been living far from people who could speak.

Language, therefore, is developed *ex novo* by the child himself. He develops it naturally, of course, but that means that he has inherited the power to do so... Yet it is the child who develops it in himself, taking it from the environment. Nothing is more interesting than the recent psychological studies based on the exact observation of the development of language in the child. Children absorb language, unconsciously of course, in a grammatical way. While they remain apparently inert for a long time, all of a sudden, within about two years and three months, they reveal a phenomenon—the explosion of a language already wholly formed.

There was, therefore, an inner development during the long period when the baby was unable to express himself. He was actually elaborating in the mysterious recesses of his unconscious mind a whole language with the grammatical order of words necessary to express thought. This children achieve with regard to all possible languages. The simple, such as those spoken by certain African tribes, and the most complicated such as German or Russian—all are absorbed in exactly the same period of time. In every race the child begins to speak at about two years of age and it was certainly so in the past also. Thus, Roman children must have spoken Latin, with its complicated cases and declensions which cause so much trouble to youths of our time who have to learn it in secondary schools. Formerly in India, small children must have spoken Sanskrit which students of today find almost insurmountably difficult.

The Tamil language of South India is very difficult for us with its almost imperceptible sounds and accents where the meaning of the sentence is changed by merely raising or lowering the voice slightly. Yet, small children of two years of age, in the villages and plains of India, speak this Tamil.

Similarly, one of the difficulties of those who study Italian is to remember the gender of nouns because not only is there no hard and fast rule governing it, but many nouns are masculine in the singular and feminine in the plural and vice versa, so it is almost impossible for a foreigner to avoid mistakes. Yet the ignorant urchins in the street never make a mistake, and laugh at those of foreigners, Sometimes learned people, who have made a real study of the Italian language and mastered all its rules and sounds, still have this remark made to them: "You have a foreign accent, what is your nationality?

Languages absorbed in early childhood are evident and inimitable. They are our "mother tongue". They are the property of the ignorant as well as of the learned. The mother tongue is a unique language for each individual who possesses it, in its sounds, its intonation and its grammatical construction. It indicates from what country one comes and to what race one belongs just as much as does the colour of one's skin or one's bodily build.

How are those different languages fixed?–those languages elaborated by infinite generations and those sounds evolved by the thought of man? Certainly not because the child gave them his conscious attention, nor because he studied them intelligently. Man has as hereditary character the faculty of speech, but it is not by heredity that any particular language is transmitted. What then is transmitted?

A comparison could be made with the nebulae from which the heavenly bodies originated. These nebulae are almost in substantial masses of ethereal gases, without consistency, which yet slowly solidify, and, transforming themselves, become stars and planets.

If, in a comparison, we supposed an inheritance of language, it would be like an inconsistent, mute nebula without which nevertheless there would be no possibility of developing any language. The nebulae are like mysterious potentialities comparable to those genes in the germinal cell which have power to direct the future tissues so that they can form complicated and structurally complete, determined organs.

The Spiritual Embryo

Could we not call the child, who in appearance only is psychically inert, an embryo, in whom the psychical powers and organs of man are being developed? He is an embryo in whom exists nothing but nebulae which have the power to develop spontaneously certainly, but only at the expense of the environment—an environment rich in greatly different forms of civilization. That is why the human embryo must be born before completing itself and why it can reach further development only after birth. Its potentialities, in fact, must be stimulated by the environment.

There will be many "inner influences" just as in physical growth there are many, especially during the processes depending on the genes, e.g. the influence of various hormones. In the spiritual embryo, instead, there are directing sensitivities. In the case of language the examination of the sense-organs reveals that the sense of hearing seems to be the least developed during the first weeks of life. Yet the most delicate sounds which compose a word have to be received through that very sense. It appears, therefore, that the ear does not merely hear as a sense-organ, but is guided by special sensitivities to collect the sounds of human speech only from the environment. These sounds are not merely heard, they provoke motor reactions in the delicate fibres of the vocal chords—the tongues, lips, etc. Thus among all the muscle fibres it is those of the speech organs which are aroused to reproduce those sounds. Nevertheless, this is not immediately revealed, but stored away till the time when language is to be born, just as the child during intra-uterine life is being formed without functioning and is then, at a given moment, stimulated to enter the world and starts functioning suddenly.

These, of course, are suppositions, but the fact remains that there are inner developments, directed by creative energies, and that these developments can reach maturity before they become outwardly manifest.

When they finally reveal themselves they are characteristics already built up to form part of the individuality of the person.

The Absorbent Mind

Certainly these complicated processes do not at all follow the procedure established in the adult mind. The child has not learned a language as we would learn a foreign tongue by an effort of our conscious mental faculties. He has yet achieved an exact, firm and marvellous construction like the embryonic constructions of an organ that forms part of a whole organism.

There exists in the small child an unconscious mental state which is of a creative nature. We have called it the "Absorbent Mind." This absorbent mind does not construct whith a voluntary effort, but according to the lead of "inner sensitivities" which we call "sensitive periods" as the sensitivity lasts only for a definite period, i.e. till the acquisition to be made according to natural development has been achieved. Thus if the nebula for language met with obstacles in its development and the constructive acoustic sensitivity did not function, a deaf-mute would be the result, though his organs of hearing and speech would be perfectly normal.

It is clear that there must be a secret fact in the psychic "creation" of man. If we learn everything through attention, volition and intelligence, how then can the child undertake his great construction as he is not yet endowed with intelligence, will-power or attention? It is evident that in him there acts a mind totally different from ours and that, therefore, a psychic functioning different from that of the conscious mind can exist in the unconscious.

The acquisition of a language can serve as the most

suitable example to give us an idea of this difference in mentality because language lends itself to study by direct and detailed observation.

The unconscious mind does not register any of the difficulties we experience with regard to different languages which make us refer to some of them as easy and to others as extremely complicated. Evidently this absence of difficulties eliminates, therefore, gradual steps in the mastery of such difficulties. The whole language is taken in and always in the same period of time, independently of its simplicity or complication, as judged by the adult mind. This total acquisition of a language cannot be compared to the effort made by the memory when we learn a language, neither need we consider the lack of retentivity of the memory which is evident in the case of the adult who easily lets his ephemeral acquisitions slip from him. In the period of unconscious activity language is indelibly stamped upon the mind and becomes a characteristic which man finds established in himself. No languaage that one may wish to add to the mother tongue can become a characteristic and none will be so sure a possession as the first.

The case is very different with the adult who has to learn a language with his conscious mind. Evidently it is quite easy to learn a primitive language with a simple grammar, like some languages of the people of Central Africa, which are often learned by missionaries during their journey across the ocean and deserts on their way to their destination. It is, on the contrary, very difficult to learn a complicated language like Latin, German or Sanskrit. Students take four, five or even eight years to study them, without knowing them perfectly even then, A living, but foreign language, is never entirely mastered—

some grammatical mistake or "foreign accent" reveals that one is not speaking one's mother tongue. Further, if this foreign language is not kept in continuous practice it is easily forgotten.

One's mother tongue is not entrusted to the conscious memory. It is deposited in a different memory similar to that which modern psychologists, biologists, and psychoanalysts call the "mneme" or "vital memory". It is supposed by some to contain what is transmitted by heredity through an infinity of time and is considered a "vital power".

A superficial comparison will, perhaps, illustrate this difference. Let us compare a photograph and a graphic reproduction made by the hand and intelligence together, in other words, by writing, drawing or painting. A camera, with its sensitive film, can in a single instant take in anything that comes to it through light. There is no greater effort involved in taking a photograph of a whole forest than in taking that of an isolated tree. A group of people and their background are as easily photographed as a single face. Whatever the complication of the figure, the camera always takes it in the same way and in the same instantaneous flash—the fraction of a second when the shutter is opened and the light-rays penetrate and reach the film. Whether one wishes to photograph the cover of a book with only its title on it, or a full page covered with fine print, it is done in the same way, takes the same length of time and produces the same result.

If, on the other hand, one wants to make a drawing this is either easy or difficult according to the subject selected. The time required to reproduce a face in profile differs greatly from that required to draw a full figure or, still more, a group of people or a landscape. A drawing, furthermore, never reproduces all the details even when we want it to do so. So much so that if a reliable document regarding a subject or the position of a body is required, a photograph and not a drawing is demanded. In the same way, to copy the title of a book is easy enough and can be done quickly but this is not the case in copying a closely-written page and as the hand works on the object the progress made shows evidence of fatigue and of the successive efforts used. But the camera, after the picture is taken, remains as before and does not show anything of what happened. To obtain the picture, the film must be taken out in a dark place, it must be exposed to chemical agents which fix the image independently of the light which produced it. Once the image is fixed, the film can be washed and exposed to light, because the image remains indelible and reproduces in all its details the object that was photographed.

It seems as if the absorbent mind acts in a like manner. There too the images must remain hidden in the darkness of the unconscious and have to be fixed by mysterious sensitivities while nothing yet appears outside. Only after this miraculous phenomenon has been accomplished will the creative acquisition be brought into the light of consciousness and there it remains indelible in all its particulars. In the case of language we witness an explosion shortly after two years of age, when the particular sounds, the prefixes and suffixes of words, their declension, the conjugation of the verbs and the syntactical construction of the sentence are all there. This is then the indelible mother tongue which has become a racial characteristic.

This absorbent mind is indeed a marvellous gift to humanity.

By merely "living" and without any conscious effort the individual absorbs from the environment even a complex cultural achievement like language. If this essential mental form existed in the adult, how much easier would our studies be. Let us imagine that we could go to another world, e.g. the planet Jupiter, and that we would find men there who by merely walking about and living absorbed all the sciences without any obvious exercises. We would surely exclaim: "How great and fortunate a miracle!" Well, this fantastic mental form does exist. The mind of the young child shows this phenomenon which has remained hidden in the mysteries of the creative unconscious.

If this happens in the case of language, the construction of sounds fashioned by man during centuries of intellectual efforts to chisel the expression of thought—it is easy to acknowledge that in a similar way the other characteristics which differentiate one race from another must be fixed in the child. These are the habits and customs, prejudices and feelings and generally all those characteristics which we feel to be incarnate within ourselves—features that are part of us independently, and even in spite of changes which our intelligence, logic and reason might be desirous of bringing about. I remember Gandhi once saying: "I could approve of and follow many customs of Western people, but I could never cancel from my soul the worship of the cow." How many may think: "Yes, my religion appears absurd according to logic, but there remains in me, and in spite of me, a mysterious feeling of devotion towards objects—a need to have recourse to them in order to live." Those people who have grown up with the impression of their taboos cannot wipe them out even when they become doctors of philosophy. The child really builds up something.

He reproduces in himself, as by a form of psychic mimesis, the characteristics of the people in his environment. Thus while growing up, he does not merely become a man—he becomes a man of his race.

With this description we have touched a psychic secret of vital importance to humanity, the secret of adaptation.

Adaptation

Adaptation as conceived by the theories of evolution would end in producing the "characteristics of the species" which differentiate them one from another, till these characteristics are fixed and transmitted unaltered by means of heredity.

Man has to adapt himself to all kinds of conditions and circumstances in the environment and never fixes himself in his habits because he evolves continuously along the course of the history of civilization. He, therefore, must possess a quick-acting "power of adaptation" which substitutes for heredity in the psychic field. This power of adaptation, although fully proved by the fact that there are men in all the geographical regions of the earth, at all latitudes and on all levels, from sea level to that of the highest mountains, does not, however, belong to the adult. The adult does not easily adapt himself, once the racial characteristics have been fixed in him. He lives well only in that particular area and feels happy only when he is immersed in an environment sharing the character-features that have been fixed in him.

The adaptation achieved by an adult who emigrates or goes to live among people with different customs is the result of an effort often quite painful. Explorers are heroes—those who live far from the centre of their life are exiles.

Once a person has adapted himself he is happy only in

his own environment, among the conditions established in his own racial group. The Eskimo feels the fascination of the Arctic environment just as the Ethiopian is attracted by the jungle. He who has lived by the sea-coast is fascinated by the jungle. He who has lived by the sea-coast is fascinated by the ocean and people of the desert enjoy the poetry of the arid and infinite plain. Those who are not adapted suffer from the effort to become so. Missionaries consider their lives in terms of sacrifice.

The child is the instrument through which everyone comes to love his own corner of the earth and becomes attached to his own customs but he is also, and for the same reason, the vehicle which transports mankind through the evolution of civilization. Every man is adapted to his own times, and lives well in them. Just as we would be unable to adapt ourselves to the social way of life of a thousand years ago, so a person of that bygone age, when there were no machines or means of rapid communication, would be unable to live amidst the noise and hurry of our day. He would be terrorized by the miracles man has accomplished by his discoveries, while we find in our environment the pleasure or, as we put it, the comforts of life.

The mechanism of this basic adaptation is simple and plain; the child incarnates in himself the environment which he finds around him, and constructs a man adapted to live in those surroundings. In order to realize this function the child lives through an initial period of psycho-embryonic construction which is found only in human beings. During this period he lives in a hidden way and is apparently an empty and inert being.

Only since the first decade of our century has the child begun to be studied. All those who have studied him have reached the conclusion that the first two years of life are the most important because during that period the fundamental features of development which characterize the human personality are established. While the newly-born possesses nothing—not even the power of voluntary movement—the child of two talks, runs, understands and recognizes things in the environment. His infancy continues further during the period of play when he organizes his unconscious creations and makes them conscious to himself.

Life is divided into well-defined periods. Each period develops properties the construction of which are guided by laws of nature.

If these laws are not respected, the construction of the individual may become abnormal, even monstrous. But if we take care of them, unknown and surprising character features—which we never even suspected—may appear. Gradually we recognize in them the inner mysterious functions which direct the psychic creation of man.

The child possesses great powers which we have not yet been able to use.

At the present stage of civilization one of the most imminent perils is that of going against nature's law in the education of the child, to suffocate and deform him under the error of common prejudices.

Contact with the World

Meanwhile, a logical conclusion follows. If the child, from birth onwards, has to create his personality at the expense of his environment, he must be brought into contact with the world, with the outward life of man. He ought to take part in, or better still, he ought to be in touch with the life of adults. If the child has to incarnate the language of his people he ought to hear them talk and be present at their conversation. If he is to adapt himself to the environment he ought to take part in public life and be a witness of the customs which characterize his race.

What a strange and impressive conclusion! If the child is a recluse in the nursery, withdrawn from social life, he will consequently be repressed, under-developed and deformed. Finally he will become abnormal and incapable of adaptation because he has been deprived of the means necessary to accomplish this great function.

Should a small child who can neither speak nor walk be brought into society, to public functions, to take part in the life of adults? Who would dare to make such a suggestion, to attempt such a profound reversal of our modern prejudices.

Even in the face of the evidence that today there is an ever increasing number of problem children, backward children, children who lack in character and initiative, children with a poor command of languages, who hesitate and stammer and grow up to be unbalanced adults suffering from psychic abnormality which obstructs their social life—and all this in spite of much hygienic care and almost continual sleep—even in the face of this evidence many people would reply: "Those things are indeed an evil, but your remedy is absurd."

Let us then have recourse to nature, because if this creative adaptation is a vital social function of the newly-born, nature must have made provision for its protection.

Well, we observe that in a natural and primitive form of life there happens exactly what we are advocating. The newly-born, the small child, the spritual embryo, who from his environment has to prepare and construct the characteristics proper to his race, always takes part in the social life of the adult. The mother carries the child in her arms and keeps him with her wherever she goes. The peasant-woman goes to the fields with her child, brings him to market or to church with her and he is present while she chats with her neighbours.

Lactation is the tie which still keeps the spiritual embryo attached to the mother. This is a fact common to all races. Even more, the very way in which mothers carry their babies, having their hands free for their work, is a characteristic trait of different people. The Eskimo mother keeps the child on her back, the Japanese mother ties him to her shoulders, the Indian mother carries him on her hip, while in some cantons in Switzerland, mothers carry their babes on their head. These mothers accomplish a second naatural function of a psychic nature. They unconsciously perform an action necessary for the salvation of the species. Mothers are anything but "revolutionaries in education". They are not teachers of their children. They do not ask them to look about or to learn. They are simply "means of conveyance". They do not at all bother about what the child observes. For them, as for everybody else, the child is an empty being, mute, incapable of intelligent activity or movement. This could almost be called a providential disposition of nature, because what the mother observes is not observed by the child and vice versa.

It is interesting to observe these facts in a primitive crowd, e.g. in a village market where there are people, animals and all kinds of objects, fruits, cloth, etc., where people discuss their affairs. There we can see how the baby who is still breast fed, this embryonic infant, looks at many things with a strangely fixed stare. He looks at the environment in its various aspects while the mother stops to do her shopping and to speak to people. The world, the environment in its totality, escapes the mother's attention but not that of the infant. The mother looks at the fruits she wants to buy; the infant is fascinated when he sees a dog or a donkey moving about. Mother and child are completely independent in their interests. The child is actually often carried by or attached in such a way to his mother that he must necessarily look in the opposite direction. Most of the mother's friends who may meet her will stop to say something nice to the baby and unintentionally give him many repeated language lessons.

In primitive races, lactation is very long—it lasts a year or even two. During all this very important period of life the child makes the conquest of the environment. It is really unnecessary for the baby that the child should be fed with its mother's milk for so long, but the mother follows an instinct of love by not detaching herself from her child, and by carrying him with her all the time though naturally his weight increases.

A French missionary, who has studied especially the customs of the Bantu people in central Africa, was astonished at the fact that the mothers do not even think of detaching themselves from their child. They consisder him as part of themselves. When attending a solemn royal installation that missionary saw the Queen arrive, child in arms, and she received the honours of a sovereign while keeping her child all the time with her. He also marvelled that Bantu women can keep up breast-feeding for so long a period. Generally it lasts two full years. In other words, it lasts for the whole epoch which nowadays is of such special interest to modern psycholgists.

These natural customs can certainly not be considered

revolutionary. We observe them with admiration and attribute to them the merit of the unperturbed character of these children who are not difficult and do not present the "problems" ours do. The secret wholly lies in two words: milk and love.

Nature, wise nature, must be the basis on which a supranature, still more perfect, can be constructed. It is certain that progress must surpass nature and adopt different forms—it may not, however, proceed by trampling upon nature.

These brief points open a practical path for those generic assertions that begin to invade our scientific world when it is said: "Education must begin at birth."

Conclusions

Man is not a vegetating body which lives only on material nourishment, nor is he destined to sensual emotions alone. Man is that superior being who is endowed with intelligence, and is destined to do a great task on earth. He must transform it, conquer it, use it and construct a new world full of marvels which surpasses and overrules the wonders of nature. It is man who creates civilization. This work is unlimited and it is the aim of his physical limbs. From his first appearance on earth, man has been a worker.

The oldest relics of man's achievement are the stones chipped by him, according to his needs which will increase and extend to infinity. He has become the dominator of all living beings, of all substances and of the very energies scattered throughout the universe. It seems, therefore, "natural to man" that the child should begin by absorbing the environment and accomplish his development by means of work, of gradual experiences in his surroundings. He nourishes and develops his human qualities first by this unconscious absorption and then by his activities directed to outward things. He constructs himself, he forms his characteristics by nourishing his spirit.

If development were limited to physical growth, the child would be condemned to a kind of hunger of the mind which could never be appeased. He would fall a victim to the grave evils of "psychic under-nourishment".

Nothing human could normally develop in him. Only a few people, so far, have discovered that the evident psychic abnormalities of modern childhood, which reveal themselves from the first years of life, are due to two things: "mental malnutrition" and "a lack of intelligent and spontaneous activity". They are due, in other words, to a repression of vital energies, destined to develop the soul of man. They are caused by a demolition of the laws which guide the growth of the child step by step.

The civilized world becomes an immense concentration camp to which all men are banished and where they are all enslaved, under-valued and annihilated in their creative impulses, withdrawn from the life-giving stimuli which every man has a right to find among those who love him.

This vague expression could be rendered concrete in the following way: "A new education from birth onwards must be built up. Education must be reconstructed and based on the laws of nature and not on the preconceived notions and prejudices of adult men."

Education today is not even based on a scientific approach to man as a whole, because nowadays a treatment of children "from birth" is being evolved which rests only on what hygiene has seen fit to prescribe as good nourishment, especially artificial food.This is facilitated by removing the mother who readily agrees that she has no more milk, isolating the child in a nursery, and entrusting him to an unknown woman who has no maternal love for him. The child is sentenced to sleep in artificial darkness provided by defending him against daylight. When he is brought out of doors, he is trailed along in a covered pram so that he sees nothing. As he is pushed along he has only the nurse in front of him and she is a kind of "infirmarian," often quite old, as it is supposed that older women are more experienced in the care of children. The affectionate looks of a beautiful young mother become something unknown to the child. He is a vegetating body. Medical specialists and psychoanalysts even dare to say that he is a "digestive tube." The silence required to make him sleep takes the place of the human voice. This "digestive tube" is very well studied. The quantity and quality of his rigorously regulated and graded food is measuced. The body is regularly weighed to follow up its growth. The caressing movements, which a mother instinctively makes on her child's limbs, are abolished, yet it is nature that inspired them for they are stimuli to life, a call towards consciousness; likewise, a delicate massage which prepares the muscles, as yet inert, by means of a passive exercise necessary when the voluntary movements have not yet been developed.

It is truly a strange situation. There is felt a terror lest the caresses of and contact with the mother should be dangerous and indecent, lest they provoke sexual instincts, in a being that has barely come into the world. But without these caresses the children may be in danger of losing their character, the power of adaptation and orientation in the complicaated world into which they are born.

It is imperative that society should awaken from

such deep-rooted errors and deliver these prisoners of misguided civilization. It must prepare for them a world adapted to their supreme needs, which are psychic needs.

One of the most urgent endeavours to be undertaken on behalf of the reconstruction of society is the reconstruction of education. It must be brought about by giving the children the environment which is adapted to their life. Well, the first environment is the world and the other environments, such as the family and the school, must correspond and satisfy those creative impulses which bring about human perfection following the guidance of the cosmic laws.

When prejudice is vanquished by knowledge, then there will appear in the world a "superior child" with marvellous powers which today remain hidden. Then there will appear the child who is destined to form a humanity capable of understanding and controlling our present civilization.

PART THREE
World Illiteracy

World Illiteracy

The question of illiteracy presents itself again these days with new vigour as a problem of great moment. It is no longer answered, as in the past,by compiling cold statistics or by drawing geographical maps showing the percentage of illiterates who, in various proportions, still exist in the countries of Europe and America.

Since the Second World War, social problems are studied on a scale which surpasses national and even continental boundaries, areas with a certain unformity of race and civilization, and extends to the world as a whole. As a consequence of the war, the Asian people—so-called Orientals—have entered the sphere of the social interest of those in the West who have a clear consciousness that all the people of the world are now closely connected. Some historic events, such as the independence of India and other Asian countries, and at the same time the efforts to contribute with the help of education to a universal understanding in the interest of all, place the problem of illiteracy among the great pressing questions of the day. That hundreds of millions of illiterates should still exist in the world, while in all continents the products and instruments of mechanized civilization are being spread, reveals the existence of a glaring contrast, a universal lack of balance. In fact UNESCO, which studies education as a practical means through which to establish greater harmony among all people, places the campaign against illiteracy in the forefront.

The problem of education, certainly, is not identical with that of illiteracy—indeed, it is very different. It concerns the spiritual formation and the intellectual uplift of mankind in order to adapt it to the changed conditions in the "new world" where, up till now, it still vegetates, unprepared and unconscious. This education, however, must circulate by means of literacy as trains circulate by means of a network of railways.

Thus independent India today places the education of her people among her most urgent tasks.

The problem of providing food for everybody is followed immediately by that of creating schools sfor all children and cultural institutions for adults. Eastern governments realize that illiteracy is a fundamental question in need of a solution.

A similar problem arose a century and a half ago in the nations of Europe and America. They determined that illiteracy and ignorance should be removed gradually by imparting to all a knowledge of what the English call the "three R's"—Reading, Writing and Reckoning—but especially Reading and Writing.

Great obstacles were immediately thrown in the way of this attempt, because there was no previous experience to indicate the road ahead. Many mistakes were made. Eastern countries can consider themselves fortunate since both obstacles and errors can now be avoided. The path has been traced and they can advance with rapid steps towards the desired goal.

In Europe the errors caused by inexperience in a rapid and total realization of child-education fell back on the children. They became the victims of a kind of slavery without precedent in human history.

Few people know that the first impulse to the realization of this colossal social effort was given by a revolution which initiated a new era in Europe. It marked, in fact, the beginning of the great scientific discoveries and the use of machinery on a vast scale.

The French Revolution of 1789 presented a strange phenomenon. Amidst the savage violence of a popular insurrection, the people themselves claimed that among the rights of man there should be that of the possession of a superior language—the written language. It was a strange, unprecedented claim. It had nothing to do with the reaction against an oppressive power which impoverished the people. The people, therefore, did not only ask for bread and work, as they did later, following the teaching of Marx, nor did they limit their claims to a change in the social hierarchies and political government. They revindicated the human right to be instructed in order to be in a position to avail themselves of Article XI of the Declaration of the Rights of Man and Citizen sanctioned in 1791. The Article reads: "The free communication of thoughts and opinions is one of the most precious of the rights of Man". Every citizen, therefore, may speak, write, print freely. It was certainly one of the few instances of people asking to be given an opportunity to make a new acquisition instead of asking for a decrease of work, because the acquisition thus claimed had to be made by the effort of each individual for himself, at the cost of painful labour.

This request was born of something considerably greater than the desire to break the chains of tyranny. In fact, three years were needed to establish the principles of a new social life and to overthrow the monarchy, but a century was needed to extend to all a knowledge of the written language.

Although the war-cry was "liberty," the conquest of literacy was not made through liberty, because compulsion was found to be necessary. The practical fulfilment of the colossal task was not accomplished by the destruction of a monarchy which had exploited the people. It was actually the conquest of another monarchy, that of the first French Empire. Napoleon, the paladin of the French Revolution, gave new strength to the people, and by preventing the re-establishment of old conditions led the people decisively to a new life. Under his magic touch, the French masses became a tidal wave breaking through the boundaries of centuries. His epic feats led to the only true conquest which remains to the present day, the raising of the people to an intellectual level, according to the rights of man.

With the Code of Napoleon, compulsory education made its first appearance in the legislation of the nations. And because Napoleon imposed his Code on the people of Europe, his principles of education conquered not only France, but the whole empire, in the wake of the terrible destructions of the war.

Compulsory education was established in many European states, then it passed to America and thus the slow and difficult task of eliminating illiteracy was started. All the civilized nations of those days took it up.

The education of the masses opened a new chapter in human history and it continued to be developed and expanded. It proclaimed a task requiring a mental effort from every individual, and the task was entrusted to the children.

In the first years of the 19th century the child entered history as an active factor in the progress of civilization. At the same time, however, he became a victim. The child could not understand, as did the adult, the necessity of this conquest, essential to social life. Mobilized from the age of six years, childhood only felt the sufferings of imprisonment and the slavery of being compelled to learn the alphabet and the art of writing. This was a dry and boring task, the importance and future advantaages of which he could not appreciate. Banished to a heavy desk, urged on by punishment, he had to learn under coercion, and to sacrifice not only his weak body, but also his personality.

Thus it has always been in the painful history of men. All the great conquests have been made at the cost of slavery. The great Egyptian monuments, the expansion of Rome across the seas, all required as a first necessity the sacrifice of men forced with the whip to perform the hard and monotonous labour such as carrying blocks of stone or rowing the galleys. And also for this new conquest of a higher degree of intelligence, in order to acquire the universal use of reading and writing, mankind needed slaves; these slaves were the children.

At the beginning of the 20th century a movement was started to ameliorate the conditions under which children passed their sentence of "hard labour". However much has been achieved in this line the child is nevertheless even today far from being given the consideration which his natural human rights demand.

It is not yet sufficienntly realized that the child who studies at school is a potential "man," that his value does not consist merely in serving as an instrument by means of which people will rise to a higher level of culture, reach national aims and obtain practical advantages for society. The child possesses "values of his own." If humanity must be improved, the child has to be understood better, he must be improved, the child has to be understood better, he must be respected and helped. Humanity, in fact, will remain as imperfect as it is today, if different levels of development, and the consequent lack of harmony which prevents advancement on the road of progress, persist. The succession of unfortunate events in our days proves it; it becomes, therefore, urgent and essential to cultivate the human energies in themselves.

In the countries where compulsory education is making its first appearance today, the experience of the past can be put to precious account and the start can be made from a higher level. The child must no longer be considered as a means of progress, or as a slave on whose shoulders the burden of the progress of civilization can be dumped. Education must begin with a view to helping the development of the child himself and thereby serving as an increment to the potentialities of the people.

"The needs of the child" are more than simply those of his physical life. Those of his intelligence and personality as a human being are equally urgent and much loftier. Ignorance is even more fatal to man than is under-nourishment or poverty.

Many people think that respect for the child and consideration for his psychical life means leaving the child alone, in inertia, i.e. without any mental activity. On the contrary, when the natural energies are taken as the basis, or in other words, when the plan of education follows the special psychology of the development of man, not only is rapid and extensive progress made, but an intensification of personal values is realized.

The progress of our civilization rests on a scientific basis and consequently education too must be planned on this same basis.

To learn to read and to write is the beginning of compulsory education, the foundation on which it is based; and so reading and writing are considered the first subjects to be taught. However, it is necessary to distinguish them from the rest of culture. Possession of the art of writing is not a mere skill, it represents the possession of a superior form of language added to its natural form. Written language complements spoken language and is integrated with it. Spoken language is developed naturally in every man. Without it he would be miserable, cut off from society, a deaf and dumb creature. Language is one of the characteristics which distinguish man from the animals. It is a gift of nature bestowed on him alone. It is an expression of his intelligence.

What would be the purpose of such an intelligence if man were not able to understand and transmit his thoughts? Without language how would he associate with other men to achieve a common enterprise, to perform work?

Spoken language is like a breath of air which can reach only the ear which happens to be close to it. That is why men, from remotest antiquity onwards, have looked for means to transmit their thoughts over a great distance and to fix their remembrance. Graphic signs were chiselled upon rocks or written on the skins of animals. From these attempts, through many transformations, the alphabet gradually evolved. This was an acquisition of paramount importance. "This conquest," writes Diringer, in his *The Alphabet* (Hutchinson's, London and New York, 1949) "is greater and of more importance than all others for the progress of civilization because it enables us to unite the thoughts of the whole of mankind all along the successive development of the generations. The alphabet concerns not only this outward development, but the very nature of man, because it completes the natural language by adding another form of expression to it."

If man is superior to the animals which have no articulate language, then the man who can read and write is superior to him who can only speak, and it is the man who writes who alone possesses the language necessary to the culture of our times. Written language, therefore, must not be considered merely as a subject in schools, and a part of culture. It is, rather, a characteristic of civilized man.

The civilization of our days cannot make progress among people who possess only spoken language, and illiteracy becomes, therefore, the greatest obstacle to progress.

***

By chance, I learnt recently the following bit of news. In China, besides the movements of Chiang Kai-Shek and the Communists, there is a third movement started by a young man who has dedicated his intelligence to the simplification of the Chinese script. He meets a need of his country which no one before him had fully understood. The traditional Chinese seript which is in use requires the knowledge of at least 9,000 characters. This makes it impossible to remove the ignorance of the masses. That young reformer, without introducing new ideas, new forms of government or better economic conditions or even freedom, has nevertheless acquired great popularity in China.

He is evidently a great benefactor of the Chinese people, who feel the need to take part in world progress—a progress only to be reached with the uplift of the human personality. The Chinese people feel that their first and fundamental right is that of possessing the two languages necessary for civilized man. The two languages are the starting point. Culture will come later.

It is, therefore, necessary to realize these points in the schools: on the one hand, the two languages connected with the formation on man—on the other, culture to be acquired at a second stage.

In view of this, I shall outline the experience gathered from the study of children, as this can be of great advantage to those who are striving to eliminate illiteracy. Written language can be acquired much more easily by children of four years than by those of six years of age—the time at which compulsory education usually starts. While children of six years of age need at least two years to learn how to write, and do so with much difficulty and against nature, children of four years learn this second language within a few months.

Not only do they acquire it without pain or effort, but with great enthusiasm. A phenomenon which, more than forty years ago, kindled in me the desire to dedicate my life to education was the spontaneous phenomenon of the "explosion of writing" in children of four years of age.

This fact, which I shall try to illustrate below, has an immense importance of practical value. If, indeed, so-called compulsory education begins with illiterate children of six years of age, they meet with great difficulties, because at that period of life it is a waste of time and energy to learn writing and reading, and this imposes upon children an arid mental effort which breeds a certain disgust towards study and all intellectual instruction.

It takes away the appetite for knowledge before one has even begun to nourish oneself with it. When instead, children of six years of age already know how to read and write, the school can immediately begin by imparting culture in an easy and interesting way and the children enter the field of study with enthusiasm.

The difference is fundamental. Really rational and modern schools capable of achieving advances in the people must be able to count upon these new children—on those who already possess the two languages—on the children of the superior man who is adapted to live in our time.

All schools begin by teaching reading and writing because written matter fixes human knowledge. It is, therefore, a logical procedure. As the aim of the school is to impart knowledge, it is necessary that children be given the means to make this knowledge durable. Reading and writing are the keys which can disclose the immense reserves of human knowledge, collected, fixed and accumulated in books by means of the art of writing. Yet, as I said before, the two things must be distinguished; writing which is an art in itself, and knowledge.

Writing has become accessible to all since the invention of the alphabet, which has simplified it so that it is within the reach even of children.

That invention has not merely simplified, but also humanized writing, because it has connected written language directly with spoken language and made the former a complement of the latter.

Spoken language is made up of only a few sounds because these depend on the possibilities of World Illiteracy combinations of the movements of the vocal organs which have their own limitations. these limitations are the same for the whole of mankind. In some languages only twenty-four or twenty-six essential sounds are used, in others more but the sounds are always limited. On the other hand, the combinations of these sounds, i.e. the number of words, is unlimited or practically so. A language can be enriched in words without limit. No dictionary contains them all No dictionary can contain the words one could make by combining letters and syllables according to the mathematical laws of permutations and combinations.

The alphabetically written language consists in giving a representation by means of a graphic sign to each sound composing a word. The result is that these signs are few in number, as few as the sounds. This representation has been perfectly achieved in the so-called "phonetic languages". Nevertheless, each alphabetically written language is more or less perfectly based on this simple principle. The fact that not all alphabetic scripts correspond phonetically to the spoken language is a difficulty caused by the incomplete application of the alphabet according to its meaning. This difficulty, however, could be corrected and writing would become correspondingly easier. There is, in fact, no doubt that languages and their translation in writing are still in the course of evolution. They are still on the road to perfection.

This is the reason why the learning of writing ought to begin with an analysis of the sounds of the words. That is the path to be followed.

Writing should not begin with those books used even today in ordinary schools, and which start by giving syllables and printed words—the primers.

The correct use of the alphabet in learning to write should only give the simple signs of the alphabet itself in order to put them in direct relation with the sounds they represent.

Then the combinations of the written words could derive directly from the spoken language which already exists in its entirety in the mind. This procedure is so simple that it can lead to writing as if by magic. The signs of the alphabet, in fact, are generally simple and easily shaped and they are so few that everyone can remember them.

Logical reasoning leads to the conclusion that if this procedure were applied, writing would come spontaneously and would immediately represent the whole spoken language which each one possesses.

With this key the problem of learning to write would be solved without any trouble. It would be possible, not only to learn to write in a few months, but writing would also develop spontaneously and become gradually more complete as the mind is concentrating on this exercise.

The alphabet in direct connection with spoken language—that is the way to achieve the art of writing by following an inner path. The ability to write will be acquired as a result of the analysis of the words each one possesses, and of the activity of one's own mind, which is interested in such a magical conquest.

If, instead, writing is made to start from books, hence from the capacity to read—and if such books give groups of arbitrarily chosen words which have to be learned—then the difficulties are increased. The result will be a separate language—a written language taken from without and derived from the deciphering of syllables or words without any interest.

It is as if an attempt were made to construct from without another language beginning with senseless, babbling sounds as happens in early infancy during the first year of life. The procedure followed would be similar to that used by nature when articulate speech is built up in a being without intelligence or motor capacities, as is man at birth.

If, instead, the alphabet is linked up with spoken language, the process becomes that of simply translating one's own language in graphic signs.

It is then always connected with words that have a meaning for the mind and the progress of writing takes place by a natural attraction. The language possessed then becomes twofold and persists by being fixed in a stable form. The eyes and the hand act together upon the treasure naturally accumulated by means of hearing and of the vocal organs. Yet, while spoken language is a breath which disappears into space, written language becomes a permanent object which remains fixed in front of the eye and can be manipulated and studied.

It is on account of its direct relation with the sounds of words that the alphabet represents one of the greatest inventions of mankind.

The alphabet has influenced human progress more than any other invention because it has modified man himself, furnishing him with new powers, above those of nature. It has made man the possessor of two languages: a natural and a supra-natural one. With the latter, man can transmit his thoughts to far away people. He can fix them for his descendants. He can practically huild up a treasure of the intellectual products of the whole of humanity through time and space.

"It is surprising," writes Diringer, "that the history of writing should be a Cinderella, as much to the educated as to the uneducated. This history is not a subject of study at the university, nor in secondary schools, nor in primary schools, and no important museum has ever considered it necessary to offer to the public a demonstrative exhibition on the development of writing."

(D. Diringer: *The Alphabet).*

Concentrating on other progress, man has not given sufficient attention to this magical instrument.

Writing is not identical with the alphabet. Writing consists of a series of attempts to transmit thought in a practical and permanent way. Its history goes back to thousands of years ago. At first, man tried to represent the objects of his thoughts by means of drawings; then he tried to symbolize ideas by signs, and only much later has he found a simple solution in the alphabet.

It is not the ideas that have to be represented by pictures, but the language in its component sounds, because only language can genuinely represent ideas and the contents of more elaborate thought. The alphabet permits us to do this because it translates the spoken word faithfully.

***

The function of the alphabet has not been taken into consideration in the ordinary method of teaching writing. It is presented only as an analysis of the written language, instead of what in fact it is, the faithful reproduction of the spoken language, It has remained submerged in writing and its own purpose has not been accentuated, nor does it arouse any interest.

It is, therefore, and arid beginning to a study, the purpose and advantages of which remain hidden from the mind of the child for a long time. The written language, even in perfectly phonetic languages, is taught in just the same way as the Chinese script would be taught, where there is no relation between the signs and the sounds composing a word, and which does not therefore possess the marvellous and practical simplicity of the alphabet.

Our experiment, begun in Rome in 1907 with children between 3 and 6 years of age, was, I believe, the first and only example of an attempt to teach writing by directly connecting the graphic signs of the alphabet with the spoken language without the use of books. The marvellous and unexpected result was that writing came "as an explosion" and began at once with whole words which flowed incessantly from the mind of the child. By means of their tiny hands they covered blackboards, floors, and walls with written words in an indefatigable and exalting creative activity, This astounding phenomenon occurred among children of four to four and a half years of age.

I am sure that this old experience will prove useful today in the fight against illiteracy, as it enables us to use the resources of nature,

To put writing in its real and simple aspects, i.e. to connect it directly with the spoken language, is already in itself a practical step forward and this can be applied to children as well as to adults. Writing thus becomes a form of self-expression and awakens an activity, heightened by the enthusiasm engendered by real interest, evident achievement, and the acquisition of a new power.

After the first phase which establishes writing in the individual, it becomes a talisman enabling its holder to penetrate into the ocean of culture and opens up to him, more or less widely, a new world. Books, readers and primers must, therefore, be abolished during this first period when writing is being acquired as a new form of self-expression. The alphabet then represents a key which is turned from within.

Culture proper is distinct from writing. Yet, if an illiterate man of wide experience and moral value can be imagined as existing before the invention of the alphabet, in our days it is inconceivable that such an illiterate person, whatever be his moral greatness, should take a real part in the culture characteristic of his time.

The two different aspects which can be distinguished when considering language can be of a great practical help.

The written language concerns self-expression. It is a very simple mechanism to be introduced into the personality. It can be analysed part by part and precisely this analysis is of the greatest value.

To be a man of letters, or not ignorant in the cultural sense, is not the same thing as knowing how to write.

Writing is related only to the alphabet and consequently to spoken speech and an analysis of its sounds. To be a man of letters, educated and cultured, means to have penetrated literature, which is linked up with the outer world—with books fixing images and thoughts; in other words, with reading.

Our experiences with children of four years of age (when writing can "explode" as a result of a conquest already made) were specially important. The development of language continues, in fact, up to the age of five years, and the mind during this period is in an active phase regarding everything that has to do with words.

This is the time—we might call it the "season in life"—when written language can ripen as does a fruit. The ripening of fruit depends not solely on the kind of seed sown and the preparation of the soil, but very much also on the season when it was sown.

The analysis of writing, which by its mechanism permits us to link it with spoken language by means of the alphabet, can be useful to adults as well as to children, but the favourable time is when spoken language is in the course of completing and perfecting itself spontaneously. This is the "sensitive psychic period" placed by nature in th child for this purpose. We can here really use the term "development of written language" because by placing the alphabet in contact with the sounds of the words the two languages develop, expand and are enriched as if they formed one organic whole.

The preparation of the mechanism is a natural process. Spoken language begins by prolonged babbling which makes the organs of speech function mechanically. Only at two years of age, when these movements are established, does language develop under the urge of the intelligence, which absorbs new words and continues to perfect the actual construction of language, absorbing it from the environment and the people amongst whom the child lives. There are then two different phases; one in which the mechanism (i.e. the smooth functioning of the organs of speech) is prepared by means of long exercise; and the other, an intellectual phase in which language is developed in its expressive construction.

In this second phase the alphabet can be of help to its further growth in perfection in the same way as the intelligtence in the adult is perfected by the acquisition of culture, when he knows how to read and write.

The important fact is that the alphabet and the

subsequent ability to write help the development of language in the child. As it is of real help to the natural development which takes place at this period it is absorbed with vital eagerness.

The signs of the alphabet, as we give them, embodied in separate objects which can be handled, act not only as stimuli drawing the activity of the consciousness towards the articulate language which had first been acquired unconsciously, and leading to an analysis of the sounds composing the words, but they also give to these sounds a visible shape which remains all the time before the eye.

The movable alphabet[1] is a docile instrument which the hand can move about making different combinations and constructing different words as one does with the various pieces of a puzzle. It thus guides the child to make a marvellous conquest.

What conquest could be more marvellous indeed?

Those few objects enable the child to construct all the words which he possesses, even those spoken by others. This simple intellectual exercise represents, therefore, a help to determine, perfect and consolidate the spoken language.

The basis of these exercises is evidently the analysis of words, i.e. spelling according to the sounds (not according to the artificial names of the letters). It is a completely inner exercise which permits the child to pass in review his own language in its component parts. This the child had never done before, nor could he ever do it, without the key furnished by these visible and movable signs.

The child thus discovers his own language. Each

1. The movable alphabet is part of the means of development offered by the Montessori Method. CF. *The Discovery of the Child*, by Dr. Maria Montessori.–N.O.T.

attempt to construct a word is based on an investigation and a discovery of the sounds forming the word he wishes to reproduce.

These exercises can be of interest also to the illiterate adult and it has been proved in fact that they do interest him.[1] The alphabet can be for everybody a key which leads to the exploration of one's language and arouses a new interest. Interest is awakened not merely on account of this analysis, which helps to overcome the difficulties of correct spelling in the written language, but also because it makes us aware of the fact that the letters of the alphabet are so few in number. Even though few, they can express the whole language in every form and on every occasion. If, for example, an adult knows a poem or a prayer by heart, all the words of that poem or prayer can be constructed. It is bewildering to reflect that all the books of a whole library, all the news which daily fills the pages of innumerable newspapers, are all combinations of the alphabetic signs. The conversations heard in one's environment, the speeches transmitted by the wireless, are all composed of those very same sounds represented by these few objects—the letters of the alphabet. It is easy to imagine that someone who is illiterate may find himself uplifted in spirit on becoming conscious of this. It may well be a revelation and an inspiration to him.

It is not these ideas, however, which fascinate the child, but in him vital energies are at work. Exercises with the

1. The Italian "National Union for the Struggle Against Illiteracy" asked Dr. Montessori to write a pamphlet which was published in Rome in 1951 with the title "Introduzione ad un Metodo per Insegnarce a Leggere e a Serivereagli Adulti" (Introduction to a Method to Teach Writing and Reading to Adults)–N.O.T.

alphabet give him exalting emotions because during the period of development of language there is in him a living flame that burns in an effort at creation.

In our first schools the children often held up cardboard pieces showing the letters of the alphabet, waving them in the air as if they were banners and revealing the impetus of their enthusiasm by their jubilant cries.

In my books I have mentioned children who walked about by themselves, like monks in meditation, softly analysing words saying to themselves "to make sofia you need s–o–f–i–a" (mentioning the individual sounds not names of the letters).

Once a father asked his child who attended our school: "Have you been good today?" to which the child replied with emphasis:

"Good–g–oo–d."

What had struck him was the word and immediately he analysed it into its component sounds.

The exercises with the movable alphabet place the whole language in motion. They provoke a real intellectual activity.

It should be noted, however, that in all these exercises the hand does not write. The child can build long and difficult words without ever having written, without ever having held a pen in his hand.

The exercise of composing words is only a preparation for writing. Yet in this exercise both reading and writing are potentially included. Writing, because the exercise results objectively in written words, and reading because when one looks at these words and interprets them, one reads. These continuous exercises, therefore, by means of which both spoken and written words are built up, do not only prepare the way for writing, but for correct spelling as well.

In ordinary schools words are usually incorrectly spelt when children start to write. This serious difficulty encountered in ordinary schools (in the USA there are even clinics for orthography now) is entirely solved by the word-building exercises with the movable alphabet. They prepare the way for reading, without books, and the way for writing, without actually writing.

It is, as I defined it, "written language delivered from its mechanisms".

Real writing, i.e. with the hand tracing the letters of the alphabet with a pen, is only an executory mechanism. It is so thoroughly detached from the intellectual effort in writing that written language can be produced by the typewriter and printing press. The hand is a kind of living machine, the movements of which have to be prepared so that they may render service to the intelligence. This preparation is given by separate exercises which firmly establish the necessary motor coordination.

The intelligence and the executive organ—here we have another distinction requiring different preparatory processes in practice.

While moving the objects used in our sensory exercises, the children's hands are being prepared for all the actions necessary for writing (see the method of indirect preparation for writing described in *The Discovery of the Child* by Dr. Maria Montessori).

It is then necessary only to give exact indications regarding the manipulation of the writing instruments.

The exactness of handling them gives the children a new interest. In the period of early childhood they are urged by nature itself to coordinate the movements of the hands, as is seen in their urge to touch everything, to take everything in their hands and to play with everything. The hand of the child in the "play-age" is led by life itself to lend itself to indirect preparation for writing. In that period also this child has a real passion for drawing. The immense advantage of having a "new" hand, animated by natural energies, is no longer found either in the adult or even in the child of six years.

He has by then emerged from the sensitive period for these activities, the play-age, the age for touching everything. He has, therefore, already established haphazardly the movements of his hands.

The condition of a labourer is still worse because when he learns to write he must first destroy something which the habit of labour has already fixed in his hand.

Yet precisely in view of this difficulty, it is as well also to prepare the hand of the illiterate adult by some indirect manual exercises and especially by drawing exercises. The drawing should not be free, but executed with precision with the help of some means which guide the hand and permit the person to obtain the visible result of well-executed decorative designs.

Thus we would use a kind of gymnastics to prepare the mechanisms of the hand. This preparation can be compared, in view of its goal, to the other, intellectual preparation for writing, achieved by means of the movable alphabet. The mind and the hand are prepared separately for the conquest of written language and follow different roads to the same goal.

The final act, viz. that of tracing effectively with the hand the alphabetic signs which the eye already knows, is now the only thing lacking.

The ordinary methods in use in schools consist in making the child copy letters already traced and held up before his eyes as a model. It seems logical but actually it is purposeless since the movements of the hand have no direct connection with the eyes. To see does not sufficiently help the hand to write.

Only the will is active when it tries to execute writing while looking at a model.

It is different in the case of spoken language, where hearing and the movements of articulation correspond in that mysterious and intimate relationship which is precisely one of the distinctive characteristics of the human species. In the case of writing, to copy is an artificial effort which produces a series of imperfect, wearying and discouraging attempts.

Now the hand can be prepared directly to trace the signs of the alphabet by the help of the tactile and muscular senses, not by that of sight. We have, therefore, prepared for our children letters cut out in sandpaper, and pasted on smooth cardboard. They reproduce in dimension and shape the letters of the movable alphabet. We teach the children to trace them in the same way as is followed in writing.

This is a very simple procedure which leads to marvellous results.

Thus the children stamp, so to speak, the shape of the letters on their hands. When they begin to write, spontaneously their penmanship is well nigh perfect and all children write in the same way because all have touched the same letters.

In the case of illiterate labourers the same procedure can be adopted. Any labourer is capable of tracing sandpaper letters, guided by the tactile sensitivity of his fingers. He can thus follow all the particular features of the simple designs corresponding to the letters of the alphabet.

I know that two centuries ago an artist working in the Vatican prepared adults in that way to execute penmanship. In those days books were still written by hand, as were exquisite parchment scrolls, which were works of art. Beautiful penmanship was a necessary accomplishment of specialists, but it was extremely difficult to execute the minute details of perfect writing.

That artist thought of having the models traced by his students instead of copied. He thus succeeded in training calligraphers with a rapidity and preciseness which otherwise would have required a very long period of training, and even then might not always have been successful.

It is as simple as the agg of Columbus–it is practical and logical.

And now when everything is ready, the hand can write effectively. If the mind has already gone through the exercises on word-building, then writing can "explode" all of a sudden; and immediately complete words, even whole sentences, are written as if by magic, as by a new gift of nature.

That is what happens during the famous "explosion into writing" experienced in children of four years of age. They write by reproducing the shapes they touched and therefore they write well. They also write with correct spelling, which was acquired independently by the intelligence in a previous phase.

The rapidity with which the children learn to write is astounding. In my first experiments, they came into contact with the alphabet for the first time in the month of October and already by about Christmas they were writing letters to their benefactors. Earlier even than that, they were writing their greetings to visitors on the blackboard.

It is well to remember that their hands had been prepared indirectly by long handling of the sensory apparatus, and also that the Italian language is almost perfectly phonetic and can be written entirely with only twenty-one alphabetic signs.[1]

But even with non-phonetic languages, the same phenomenon occurs, although it takes slightly longer. In countries with non-phonetic languagaes such as English, Dutch and German, children six years old were able to read and write.

Regarding reading, it is already in a sense implied in the exercise with the movable alphabet. In a perfectly phonetic language it could be developed without any further aid if there were a strong impulse to know the secrets of writing.

Our small children, on their Sunday walks with their parents, would stop for a long time in front of the shops and succeed in deciphering the names written outside, although they were in printed capital letters while they had learnt only the letters of the movable alphabet in cursive script.

They accomplished, therefore, a genuine exercise in interpretation similar to that carried out when the inscriptions of ancient people are deciphered.

---

1. The method has also been worded out successfully for Indian languages and scripts and is explained in the "Indian Montessori Training Courses" held under the auspices of the Association Montessori Internationale.

   Its practical application can be observed in India, in the AMI Montessori Houses of Children–N.O.T.

Such an effort could be evoked only by an intense interest in understanding what was written.

Once, in our first school attended by children whose parents were all illiterate and who, therefore, had no books at home, one of the children brought a piece of crumpled dirty paper saying: "Guess what this is!" "A piece of dirty paper," was the reply. "No–a story!" The other children gathered round him with the greatest astonishment and all were persuaded of the prodigious truth.

Afterwards they looked for books, and would tear the pages out of them to take them home.

This experience shows that learning to read depends more on mental activity than on teaching.

At five years of age the children read whole books, and reading afforded them as much satisfaction and entertainment as did the fairy tales and news which adults used to tell them for their amusement.

Children are interested in books when they know how to read. This is so obvious that it seems superfluous to say so.

In ordinary schools, however, reading begins directly with books. There children must learn to read by reading.

The first readers are prepared on the basis of old prejudices which see imaginary difficulties that have to be overcome successively.

At the beginning, short words are given, then longer ones. First simple, then complex syllables, and so on, are presented. In other words, obstacles are placed in front of the child at every step.

But these difficulties do not actually exist. The children already know short and long words and all kinds of syllables in their mother tongue. All that is necessary is to analyse the sounds and find the corresponding alphabetic sign for each. That is all—although it may seem difficult for one who is unfamiliar with this truth to understand it. Reading should not be used to overcome difficulties such as those mentioned here.

Reading is the entrance by means of the written language to the field of culture. It is not, like writing, a means of speaker. Such reflective exploration of the verb also awakens in the consciousness a notion of the different latitudes of time. The irregular verbs, otherwise so difficult to learn, exist already in the language spoken by the child and it is now only a question of "discovering" that they are irregular.

All this is different when one has to study a foreign language, where everything has to be learned anew.

But is the grammar of one's mother tongue not also studied in ordinary schools?

There the mother tongue is actually studied as if it were a foreign language.

The divine and mysterious work of creation, the greatest miracle of nature, is ignored and passed over.

***

It is easy to understand that these grammatical reading exercises in all their simplicity and clarity can also be used for illiterate adults.

Otherwise, in order to learn to read, they would have to make the effort of understanding what is written in books which have no attraction whatever, because of the monotonous uniformity of their printed type. They require the knowledge of two different alphabets at the same time, the written and the printed scripts, and that is an additional difficulty

The grammatical exploration of language not only helps reading, but also provides stimulus and satisfaction because it renders conscious the language one already possesses. To read books, on the other hand, compels us to concentrate on thoughts coming from without.

Besides, in practice, it is not easy to find many teachers who are willing to teach a mass of illiterate adults and who themselves possess a thorough knowledge of grammar. Material which is prepared and ready for use can make up for the imperfections of improvised teachers, while rendering teaching easier for the teachers themselves.

In relation to an experiment undertaken in Great Britain after the Second World War, a Scottish teacher said: "I was embarrassed with all the things I had to do, but the apparatus made up for my insufficiency. The class has become a real grammar factory in which all the labourers are busy and cheerful."

***

Culture in itself, as I said earlier, must not be confused with learning to read and write.

The five-year-old child is cultured not because he possesses written language, but because he is intelligent and will have learnt many things.

In fact, our children at six years of age already possess much varied knowledge in biology, geography, mathematics, etc. which they gain from direct contact with visible apparatus that can be manipulated.

But that is a subject different from what I wished to deal with here. I intended to deal only with one subject of great immediacy, the elimination of illiteracy among the masses.

Culture can be transmitted by means of the spoken

word, also by the radio and phonographic records. It can be passed on by the help of projections and films. Above all, however, it has to be taken in through activity with the help of apparatus which permits the child to acquire culture by himself, urged onwards by the nature of his mind which seeks and is guided by the laws of his development. These laws prove that culture is absorbed by the child through individual experience, by the repetition of interesting exercises which always require the contribution of the activity of the hand, the organ which cooperates with the development of the intelligence.